**New Directions for
Teaching and Learning**

Marilla D. Svinicki
EDITOR-IN-CHIEF

Designing Courses for Significant Learning:
Voices of Experience

L. Dee Fink
Arletta Knight Fink

EDITORS

Number 119 • Fall 2009
Jossey-Bass
San Francisco

DESIGNING COURSES FOR SIGNIFICANT LEARNING: VOICES OF EXPERIENCE
L. Dee Fink, Arletta Knight Fink (eds.)
New Directions for Teaching and Learning, no. 119
Marilla D. Svinicki, Editor-in-Chief

Microfilm copies of issues and articles are available in 16mm and 35mm, as well as microfiche in 105mm, through University Microfilms, Inc., 300 North Zeeb Road, Ann Arbor, MI 48106-1346.

NEW DIRECTIONS FOR TEACHING AND LEARNING (ISSN 0271-0633, electronic ISSN 1536-0768) is part of The Jossey-Bass Higher and Adult Education Series and is published quarterly by Wiley Subscription Services, Inc., A Wiley Company, at Jossey-Bass, 989 Market Street, San Francisco, CA 94103-1741. Periodicals postage paid at San Francisco, CA, and at additional mailing offices. POSTMASTER: Send address changes to New Directions for Teaching and Learning, Jossey-Bass, 989 Market Street, San Francisco, CA 94103-1741.

New Directions for Teaching and Learning is indexed in CIJE: Current Index to Journals in Education (ERIC), Contents Pages in Education (T&F), Current Abstracts (EBSCO), Educational Research Abstracts Online (T&F), ERIC Database (Education Resources Information Center), Higher Education Abstracts (Claremont Graduate University), and SCOPUS (Elsevier).

SUBSCRIPTIONS cost $98 for individuals and $267 for institutions, agencies, and libraries in the United States. Prices subject to change.

EDITORIAL CORRESPONDENCE should be sent to the editor-in-chief, Marilla D. Svinicki, Department of Educational Psychology, University of Texas at Austin, One University Station, D5800, Austin, TX 78712.

www.josseybass.com

CONTENTS

FROM THE SERIES EDITOR

About This Publication

Since 1980, *New Directions for Teaching and Learning* (NDTL) has brought a unique blend of theory, research, and practice to leaders in postsecondary education. NDTL sourcebooks strive not only for solid substance but also for timeliness, compactness, and accessibility.

The series has four goals: to inform readers about current and future directions in teaching and learning in postsecondary education, to illuminate the context that shapes these new directions, to illustrate these new directions through examples from real settings, and to propose ways in which these new directions can be incorporated into still other settings.

This publication reflects the view that teaching deserves respect as a high form of scholarship. We believe that significant scholarship is conducted not only by researchers who report results of empirical investigations but also by practitioners who share disciplines reflections about teaching. Contributors to NDTL approach questions of teaching and learning as seriously as they approach substantive questions in their own disciplines, and they deal not only with pedagogical issues but also with the intellectual and social context in which these issues arise. Authors deal on the one hand with theory and research and on the other with practice, and they translate from research and theory to practice and back again.

About This Volume

Sometimes, after hearing about a really great idea or system for teaching, one of the hardest things to do is to turn the rhetoric into one's own practice. This volume shows how teachers from a wide range of disciplines implemented the idea of integrated course design in order to design significant learning experiences. Their stories show others that it can be done.

Marilla D. Svinicki
Editor-in-Chief

MARILLA D. SVINICKI is the director of the Center for Teaching Effectiveness at the University of Texas at Austin.

PREFACE

My book *Creating Significant Learning Experiences* (2003) is a combination
of a new vision of what teaching and learning could be and a synthesis of
many ideas in the literature on college teaching. It also draws extensively
from my experience helping faculty members redesign their courses. However, because the ideas were new, not many people had tried them yet.

That situation has since changed. I have conducted workshops on integrated course design (ICD) for several years, as have others, both nationally
and internationally. As a result, a significant number of professors have used
these ideas to design and redesign their courses, with extremely positive
results. Every now and then I get an e-mail from someone saying, in
essence, "You have changed my life as a teacher. I can see more clearly what
I want my students to learn, and I now have the tools to get that kind of
learning to happen."

Therefore, we are now in a position to share stories about ICD. Hearing their stories will allow all of us to see, in much richer detail than I was
able to offer at the time my book came out, how different people are applying these ideas in multiple contexts and what happens when they do.

The Essential Ideas of Integrated Course Design

The basic premise of my book is that any student who takes a course has an
experience. Sometimes that experience is powerful; at other times it is trite.
Every teacher who cares about his or her students' learning wants that experience to be on the powerful and significant end of that spectrum.

When we want students to have a significant learning experience, we
have to answer two questions. First, what might we mean by a "significant
learning experience"? And second, how can we intentionally teach in a way
that gives students that kind of experience more often? My book offers ways
of answering both questions. A summary of those answers follows.

What Is a Significant Learning Experience?

This question has both a process and a product way of answering it. Figure
P.1 illustrates the process view.

During the course, we want students to be *engaged*. This means they
do the preclass homework assignments, come to class, pay attention, participate in class activities, and so forth. That is, they spend the energy necessary to do the work of learning. But we want this process to lead to a
product; by the end of the course, we want them to have learned something

NEW DIRECTIONS FOR TEACHING AND LEARNING, no. 119, Fall 2009 © Wiley Periodicals, Inc.
Published online in Wiley InterScience (www.interscience.wiley.com) • DOI: 10.1002/tl.358

Figure P.1 Features of a Significant Learning Experience

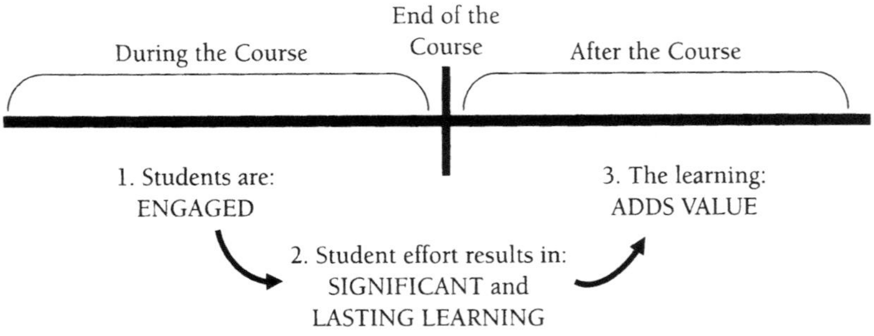

End of the
Course

During the Course   After the Course

1. Students are: 3. The learning:
   ENGAGED   ADDS VALUE

2. Student effort results in:
   SIGNIFICANT and
   LASTING LEARNING

that is significant and that lasts. We also want that which the students have learned by the end of the course, to be something that adds value to their personal, professional, social, or civic lives after the course and after college.

We want all three parts of this process to happen. My belief is that if we focus on and can get the second component (significant learning by the end of the course) to happen, that will greatly increase the likelihood of the other two happening. This leads to the product view of significant learning, which is where the taxonomy of significant learning comes in. This taxonomy, shown in Figure P.2, offers a new way of identifying a wide range of desired learning outcomes.

These goals are not just individually valuable and accumulative; they are interactive. This means the more you can get all of them to happen, the easier it is to get any one of them to happen well.

Like other taxonomies of learning, this one can be used to formulate learning goals and find ways of assessing different kinds of learning. If we use this taxonomy to formulate a generic set of learning goals, they might look like this:

By the end of this course, my hope is that students will . . .

1. Understand and remember the key concepts, terms, principles, facts, and so forth.
2. Be able to use the content.
3. Be able to relate this subject to other subjects.
4. Identify the personal and social implications of knowing about this subject.
5. Value this subject—as well as value further learning about the subject.
6. Know how to keep on learning about this subject after the course is over.

One of the values of the chapters in this book is seeing what happens when teachers in different disciplines use this taxonomy to create course-specific learning goals.

Figure P.2 Taxonomy of Significant Learning

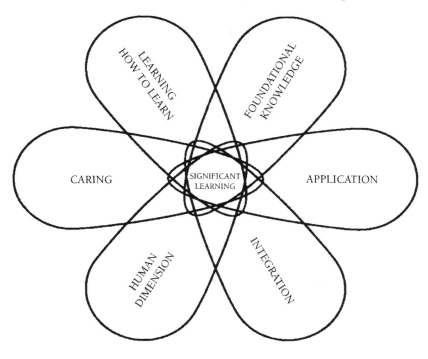

How Do We Get Significant Learning to Happen More Frequently and More Intentionally?

The taxonomy of significant learning allows us to imagine a more exciting set of possibilities for what students might learn in our courses. But then we have to figure out how to make it happen. The ICD model provides a conceptual framework for working on this task. In my book, I identify twelve steps in the full course design process, but the core of that process is shown in Figure P.3.

This model indicates that the task of designing any learning experience begins by focusing on five components:

1. *Situational factors:* We start by gathering information about important variables that should be taken into consideration; for example, the number of students, the time structure, students' prior knowledge and attitudes toward the subject, expectations that other stakeholders have for what students learn in this course, the nature of the subject, and so forth. We use this information to make three major decisions, and the first of these must be about the learning goals.

Figure P.3 Integrated Course Design Model

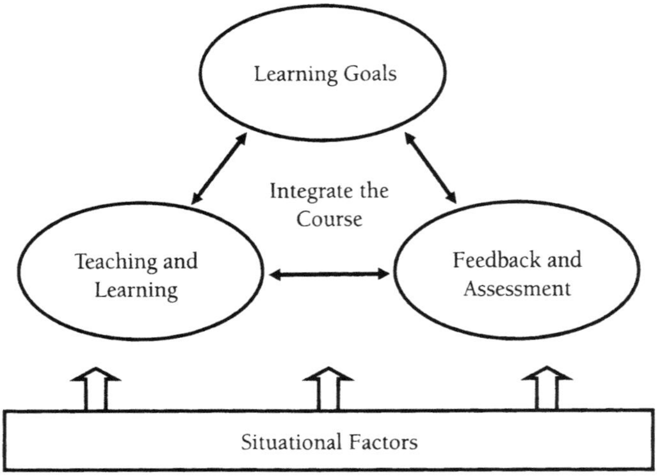

2. *Learning goals:* We have to identify what we want students to learn in this course. By doing this first and then basing the next two decisions on the learning goals, we make the course learning centered. The taxonomy of significant learning can be helpful in this process.
3. *Learning activities:* Once we know what we want students to learn, we can address the question of how they will learn that. In other words, what learning activities will be necessary to enable students to achieve our desired learning goals? The concept of active learning can help us select a good set of learning activities.
4. *Feedback and assessment activities:* We must decide what students need to do, which will allow both teacher and students to know whether they have learned what was intended. The concept of educative assessment offers a good set of principles to help in this process.
5. *Integrating the course:* Using a three-column table and a good teaching strategy can help with the task of making the course integrated.

Figure P.4 provides a macroview of the process of working on these components of ICD.

1. Build a good set of learning goals, perhaps using the taxonomy of significant learning.
2. Put the learning goals in the left-hand column of the three-column table.
3. For each learning goal, use the three-column table to identify appropriate learning activities and assessment activities, applying the principles of active learning and educative assessment.

Figure P.4 General Sequence of Integrated Course Design

LEARNING IMAGINED ▬ ▬ ▬ ▬ ▬ ▬ ▬ ▬ ➔ **LEARNING ACHIEVED**

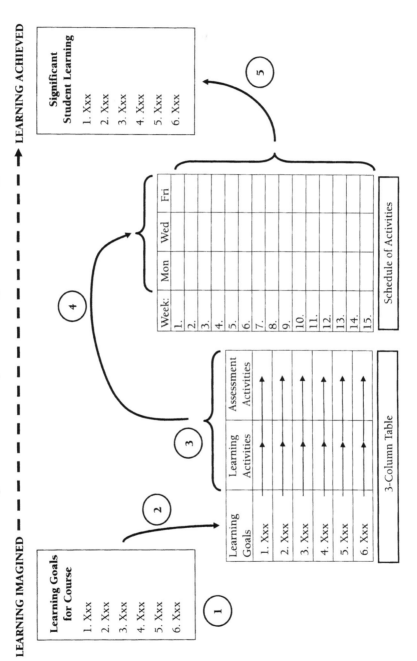

4. Put the learning and assessment activities into your schedule of activities. All have to be in there somewhere in order to drive the kind of learning you want. But as you put them in, pay attention to the combination and sequence of the activities, that is, your teaching strategy.
5. If you have done a good job on each of the preceding steps, the set of course experiences will result in something close to the kind of learning you had imagined initially: significant learning for your students.

These ideas have now been used by professors in multiple disciplines and in many countries around the world. Several of these teachers describe their experiences in this volume.

The Chapters

When I invited people who had used ICD to write a chapter for this volume of *New Directions for Teaching and Learning*, many more offered to do so than I could include here. Faced with a surplus and the necessity of making choices, I tried to select authors who:

- Had implemented the ideas of ICD well.
- Had evidence of its impact on improving student engagement and learning.
- Represented a range of teaching situations. This included people teaching different kinds of subject matter, in different kinds of institutions, and applying the ideas in the design of programs as well as in individual courses.

After making the difficult choices, I asked the authors to write about their experiences and organize their comments around four questions:

- Why did you decide to make changes in your teaching?
- What did you change in the design of your course?
- What was the impact of the new course design on student learning, student engagement, or your teaching?
- What lessons did you learn from the whole change effort?

The chapters in this volume were chosen in part to show what happens when the ideas of significant learning and ICD are applied to different kinds of subject matter and teaching situations. Therefore, the chapters address several kinds of subject matter:

- Natural sciences: Virology (Chapter Eight, by Joseph C. Mester) and biology, anatomy, and physiology (Chapter Five, by Carolyn Fallahi and others)
- Social sciences: Economics (Chapter Three, by Lawrence Miners and Kathryn Nantz) and life span development and early childhood (Chapter Five, by Carolyn Fallahi and others)

- Humanities: Spanish (Chapter Two, by Debra Dimon Davis), music (Chapter Four, by Bruce C. Kelley), and art history and philosophy (Chapter Seven, by Marice Rose and Roben Torosyan)
- Professional schools: Accounting (Chapter One, by Marsha M. Huber), engineering (Chapter Ten, by Randall L. Kolar, David A. Sabatini, and K. K. Muraleetharan), education (Chapter Six, by Harriet R. Fayne, and Chapter Nine, by Joan M. Nicoll-Senft)

Most of the chapters describe undergraduate courses taught in face-to-face settings at four-year institutions. However, some were taught in other settings:

- A community college (second-year Spanish, Chapter Two)
- A hybrid course (special education, Chapter Six)
- A graduate course ("Preparing for College-Level Teaching," Chapter Eleven; special education, Chapter Nine)
- A curricular project ("Sooner City Project," Chapter Ten)

Arletta Fink agreed to edit the chapters and to help write a concluding chapter that summarizes what we can learn from these voices of experience. She performed these same tasks extremely well when she worked with Larry Michaelsen and me as a coeditor of Michaelsen's book *Team-Based Learning* (2004). So I asked her to do the same thing here. Her effort has been very beneficial and greatly appreciated.

L. Dee Fink
January 2009

References

Fink, L. D. *Creating Significant Learning Experiences: An Integrated Approach to Designing College Courses.* San Francisco: Jossey-Bass, 2003.

Michaelsen, L. K., Knight, A. B., and Fink, L. D. (eds.). *Team-Based Learning: A Transformative Use of Small Groups in College Teaching.* Sterling, Va.: Stylus, 2004.

L. DEE FINK founded and directed the Instructional Development Program at the University of Oklahoma from 1979 until 2005. He currently works as a national and international consultant on instruction in higher education.

1

The author used the integrated course design model to create new learning activities in her course on federal taxation. Although she is a veteran teacher, she found this new way of thinking about her courses unleashed her creativity and set her on a path of continuous learning.

Shoeboxes and Taxes: Integrated Course Design Unleashes New Creativity for a Veteran Teacher

Marsha M. Huber

In December 2005, I attended a workshop presented by Dee Fink sponsored by my institution, Otterbein College. I had not heard of Fink prior to the workshop, and so I did not know what to expect from the seminar. In fact, at that time, I was not familiar with the literature on instructional design. Although I hate to admit it, it was more the offer of the free lunch and book that brought me to the workshop rather than the subject matter. The seminar, however, introduced me to a teaching pedagogy that would not only change how I taught but would transform my career as an accounting educator.

After Fink introduced the six dimensions of learning—foundational knowledge, application, integration, caring, the human dimension, and learning how to learn—I realized I was teaching in only two of the six dimensions. As an accounting educator, I focused on foundational knowledge and application and had not heard of, let alone considered, the other four dimensions. The idea of developing caring and learning how to learn was especially intriguing to me since my discipline did not normally lend itself to supporting those particular dimensions.

With twenty years of teaching experience, I considered myself a decent accounting teacher. I had not thought of teaching as a craft that needed to be developed and perfected over time. The evening following the seminar, I decided to test Fink's concepts and redesigned my courses for the upcoming term.

New Directions for Teaching and Learning, no. 119, Fall 2009 © Wiley Periodicals, Inc.
Published online in Wiley InterScience (www.interscience.wiley.com) • DOI: 10.1002/tl.359

If his theory worked, maybe something spectacular could happen in my classes.

As the evening progressed, I struggled to write new learning goals and congruent learning experiences for all six dimensions of learning. I kept referring to my workshop notes and Fink's book, *Creating Significant Learning Experiences* (2003), to figure out how to properly redesign my courses. Once I was satisfied with my revamped courses, I sent my new syllabi to the director of Otterbein's teaching and learning center for her feedback.

I could hardly contain my excitement as I told my colleagues about the redesign the next day. Would these changes work? Would I see improvements in student learning? Could the mundane be transformed into something exciting simply through course redesign?

The Changes I Made Based on Integrated Course Design

I began making changes to my courses by first setting learning goals and then creating learning experiences that allow those goals to be accomplished. Follow-up assessments of such learning experiences provides a way to evaluate and improve classes.

Setting Learning Goals

My initial attempt to redesign my courses seemed rudimentary. Initially I set up a table listing each learning goal with its corresponding learning experience, and assessment technique. I used action verbs from Fink's book to describe each goal. Table 1.1 represents my first attempt at revising my Individual Taxation course. This course, taken primarily by accounting and finance majors, covers the impact of federal tax law on individuals.

It was a good start; nevertheless, I modified the syllabus for the following quarter. I incorporated the ideas from Table 1.1 into a new syllabus with a more student-friendly format. For example, the human dimension was presented as "Engage in critical evaluation of tax issues/implications that you encounter in the public media: You will critique three YouTube videos on current events in the public press for accuracies and inaccuracies. The quality of your critique will be assessed." And the learning-how-to-learn dimension became "Being responsible for your own learning is a key to your success in the future: You will create a course portfolio to reflect your learning and giving evidence of your best and worst class work."

The new syllabus format still reflected all six learning dimensions, but without the table. I wanted to write a syllabus that students could easily read to prepare them for what awaited them during the term.

Creating Learning Experiences

When redesigning the course, I needed to create learning experiences to support learning goals in the dimensions that were new to me. This was my greatest challenge, especially in a tax course that was so quantitative. As I

Table 1.1 Three-Column Table for Federal Income Taxation Course

Learning Goals	Learning Experiences	Assessment
Foundation knowledge: Understand and remember key concepts and terms.	Read the text, lecture, and use Pub. 17.	Quizzes and tests
Application: Use the concepts to solve complicated and ambiguous tax problems.	Solve tax return problems and case studies.	Complexity of thought; correctness
Integration: Identify the interaction between tax law and personal, societal, and business decisions.	Interview your parents and a businessperson to discuss the impact of tax law on decision making. Develop models.	Presentation of group model to the class
Human dimension: Become aware of the impact of taxes on society as a whole.	Engage in a critical analysis of tax issues that you encounter in the public media, such as Bush's tax plan. Be aware of ethical standards that guide CPAs.	Critiques of articles in the public media; case studies
Caring: Become confident in your ability to apply course material to real-world situations.	Complete a tax return for a friend, and develop a "shoebox" case that another team will solve.	Peer evaluation and realistic nature of the case
Learning how to learn: Reflect on your learning.	Write reflection papers throughout the term.	Depth of reflection

thought about what I wanted my students to be able to do at the end of the course, I realized that many of my prior assignments promoted passive rather than active learning. My students were not doing or creating; they were merely responding to whatever I gave them. In redesigning the course, I swapped active learning experiences for passive ones. For example, instead of inviting a guest to speak to my students about the tax profession, with my students acting as observers, I asked the students to interview professionals about how taxes have an impact on business decision making. Using their individual interviews, the students developed models with their teammates about what they learned. Based on criteria they developed, the students then selected the best model. This exercise emphasized both foundational knowledge, since students learned terminology from the businesspeople, and caring, since students learned how the course material would be relevant to their futures as taxpayers and professionals.

My focus on active learning also helped me think in new ways about possible learning and assessment activities. I previously thought that having students work on a lengthy case study (that I had written) represented an excellent final project. My students, however, did not share my enthusiasm. In fact, many of them despised the project, putting forth minimal effort to solve the case study.

The Shoebox Exercise

With my new perspective, I decided a more realistic assignment might be better—perhaps a shoebox case, that is, a simulation where students are given realistic documents to use in preparing a tax return. Then it occurred to me: "Why should I develop the case? Why don't I have the students create documents for their own case, put them in a shoebox, swap them, and prepare the tax return for the case they received?"

The shoebox case gave my students an opportunity to construct new knowledge. This activity supported the dimensions of application, caring, and learning how to learn. Furthermore, students learned to apply content from the class as they created their shoeboxes, researched to find information and source documents for the case, and gained confidence in tax preparation as they developed their cases and solved another team's case. The students were enthusiastic and competitive as they created an original, comprehensive, and challenging case for another team to solve.

Improving My Course Redesign

Since 2006, I have steadily worked to improve my courses. I found that although my learning goals remained constant, the learning experiences sometimes needed to be revised. One way I gauged the effectiveness of the learning experiences was to ask my students to rate the learning experiences in the course. Table 1.2 represents an abbreviated mockup of the rating system that I used twice each term.

The rating system has helped me to decide which learning experiences needed to be revised over time. For example, my students rated an assignment that required them to critique an article in the public media as low. In

Table 1.2 Reflection Paper (Ranking Portion)

How helpful were the following for your learning?	High	Good	Average	Low	Not at All
Working in groups in class	5	4	3	2	1
Reading the text	5	4	3	2	1
Doing short homework problems in the book	5	4	3	2	1
Lectures	5	4	3	2	1
Course portfolio	5	4	3	2	1
Clickers	5	4	3	2	1
Online quizzes	5	4	3	2	1
The YouTube videos	5	4	3	2	1
Developing the shoebox case	5	4	3	2	1

response, I replaced that assignment with a set of structured questions about three preselected YouTube videos. The students rated this new learning experience as high.

The rating system also has helped me differentiate how situational factors affect student learning. For example, my traditional accounting class rated the usefulness of clickers at a 4.4 but lectures at 3.8, whereas my adult evening class reported opposite ratings, with clickers at 3.1 and lectures at 4.6. Based on the results, I still use the clickers in the traditional classes, but not in my evening sections, thereby allowing more time for lecture.

No doubt my courses have been transformed by integrated course design over the past three years. I am now in the process of reevaluating my grading schemes for fairness. I recently discovered that even with the redesign, my point allocation still favored foundational knowledge and application, comprising 60 to 70 percent of the grade. I had to add projects to my courses, such as a learning portfolio to the tax class, to shift more points to the learning-how-to-learn dimension. To truly improve teaching and student learning, the revision process must be continuous.

Impact on Student Engagement and Learning

Overall the results of the course redesign have been encouraging. A tax student who experienced the transition of my courses (before and after the redesign) wrote:

> This has been one of the best classes I've taken at Otterbein. . . . I will be able to use the knowledge in the future. I like the new way you conducted your class. It gives the students a much better understanding of the information presented to them. We do not have to get so worked up about exams and cram the night before only to forget the info the next day.

Another student commented:

> I was surprised the class wasn't all about lectures, tests, and notes. The projects you assigned helped me learn the material way better than any lecture could ever do. I appreciate the fact that tests aren't weighed as much as they usually are. Students will not remember most of the information after leaving the class; it's the projects and discussions that I will remember. . . . I like your new "teaching method" as opposed to the traditional classes. . . . You created a good environment and people were able to exchange ideas.

Qualitative indicators of student learning revealed that students were not only learning the course material, but were also developing professional mind-sets (part of the caring dimension). One student expressed gaining confidence in solving "real-world" problems: "The interesting thing that I learned is how to do somebody's taxes (the shoebox case) without my professor's help." Another student showed improved self-assurance: "The thing that surprised me was that I enjoyed and remembered why I am majoring in accounting. . . . I am confident that accounting is where I belong." Furthermore, some were gaining perspective on the accounting profession: "I have more respect for the career I am pursuing. Being an accountant is an all day job. You don't really leave your work at the office. . . . I will have to be always ready for whatever a client brings to my office."

Even last term, the depth of responses regarding the new course portfolio impressed me. At first students expressed skepticism, but they changed their minds as they worked on the portfolios:

> Doing the portfolio was difficult in the beginning because I did not believe it would be a valuable experience. I found myself arguing with myself, "I don't have time to do this because I need to learn all the details of actual work." I overcame my initial reluctance, emotionally through trust in my professor, intellectually by the knowledge that it was course requirement and would help me with my job, and personally by the fact that once I started the project I found it helpful to organize my thoughts and rewarding to see visually how I was progressing and learning.

The course portfolio enhanced the learning-how-to-learn dimension, and even developed caring:

> It was hard to get started . . . but once I did, ideas kept popping in my head allowing me to write this portfolio piece much faster than I thought I would be able to do. I think this is a very good exercise. I think I may have appreciated other classes more had I been forced to think about these different questions. I may have realized why all the students are required to take a course or how the information might have helped them in the future.

Lessons Learned

Fink's integrated course design has had a pervasive influence not only on my teaching but on my career. Before I adopted this approach, my work reflected that of a typical accounting educator. After the redesign, I began to develop as a scholar in my own right.

My Otterbein colleagues encouraged me to share publicly what I was doing in my courses. Because of their suggestions, I began to teach seminars on using Fink's approach in accounting classes at the regional and national meetings of the American Accounting Association (AAA). As my reputation as a scholar spread, I began receiving invitations to speak and write. This year, I was asked to write two articles for a monograph for the AAA on measuring learning. In addition, I was invited to be a keynote speaker and a plenary speaker, and I will be a featured presenter at an upcoming international

Lilly Conference. I was also selected as a CASTL scholar (Carnegie Academy for the Scholarship of Teaching and Learning) for a more unconventional paper, "Emancipatory Action Research in Accounting." Finally, I received a grant with a colleague to investigate using blogs and wikis to improve students' reflective and critical thinking skills.

As I study and write about the scholarship of teaching, I am driven by a new-found passion. The more I learn, the more I realize how much I do not know about this topic. To continue my development as a scholar, I returned to graduate school, where I am taking classes in cognitive theories and qualitative research. The use of Fink's paradigm of significant learning has opened a door of discovery for me.

The unexpected reward for me is not so much the accolade from others, but the changes that have taken place within me and in my courses. I have found a joy in teaching. It is gratifying to watch my students experience greater success in their learning as a result of the course redesign. Over the past three years, my passion for teaching has been invigorated as I hone my craft, serve as a mentor to other educators, and mature as a scholar in my discipline.

Reference

Fink, L. D. *Creating Significant Learning Experiences: An Integrated Approach to Designing College Courses.* San Francisco: Jossey-Bass, 2003.

MARSHA M. HUBER is a professor of accounting and administrative dean's fellow at Otterbein College in Westerville, Ohio. E-mail: mhuber@otterbein.edu.

NEW DIRECTIONS FOR TEACHING AND LEARNING • DOI: 10.1002/tl

*Concerned that her students "knew" Spanish but could
not use it in real life situations, Davis created new learning goals, new learning activities, and new assessment
activities. Result? New kinds of significant learning.*

Bringing Language to Life in Second-Year Spanish

Debra Dimon Davis

Six people are seated around a table in a small Mexican restaurant. As they enjoy the fresh tortilla chips and homemade salsa, they are studying the menus with more than the usual attention to detail. The waitress is speaking Spanish. The patrons at this table are doing their best to understand what she is saying and are making an effort to place their orders in Spanish as well.

At a glance, this could be any group of friends enjoying a cultural dining experience, but these customers are the members of a Spanish class who are putting their classroom learning to a practical test.

The Need for Changes

Teaching Spanish classes at the community college continually presents new challenges. My students vary in age from the sixteen-year-old dual-credit high school student to a seventy-two-year-old retiree, and they represent lifestyles and career goals as different as the recipes for good salsa. Standard teaching methods of the one-size-fits-all variety fall short in this context. Textbooks designed for traditional college-age students may not be as effective for older adult learners. Students who have never before studied a foreign language are often fearful of speaking in front of others. Many students of Spanish complain that despite the amount of time they spend in class, they have little to show for their effort and are unable to

speak the language. This breakdown between classroom learning and active language use indicates a need for a new look at learning goals and teaching methods in foreign language instruction. What would I need to change in order for this learning experience to be relevant and applicable for these diverse students?

As a graduate student at the University of Illinois, I was introduced to *Creating Significant Learning Experiences* (Fink, 2003) while studying with Steven Aragon in the community college teaching and learning program. Aragon began his course on program development by asking, "What do you dream for your students?" This startling question from the opening paragraph of Fink's book caused me to rethink the learning goals for my Spanish class. What did I dream for my students? The restaurant scenario came to mind. I wanted my students to be able to use their Spanish language skills in the world outside the classroom.

My design for a new Spanish course began as a project for Aragon's class and became a reality when a group of my beginning Spanish students requested a tutorial with me as an alternative to the traditional second-year Spanish class.

The model I used to design my course was Dee Fink's taxonomy of significant learning. I began by examining situational factors related to the course and then moved on to setting learning goals, creating teaching and learning activities, and developing methods for feedback and assessment.

Learning Goals

My previous course goals for second-year Spanish had been textbook driven and consisted of memorizing the grammar and vocabulary material presented in a given number of chapters. I revised the learning goals for my new course to include more active use of this memory work. For example, what did I actually want my students to be able to do after completing this course? If the students could use Spanish with native speakers outside the classroom, my objectives for real-world contexts would be met.

I drew my learning goals from the six kinds of significant learning that Fink (2003) described: foundational knowledge, application, integration, the human dimension, caring, and learning how to learn. The three types of learning were familiar concepts and required only a revision of previous goals, but learning goals involving the human dimension, caring, and learning how to learn were new to me. Table 2.1 compares some original and redesigned course goals.

Teaching and Learning Activities

I designed new teaching and learning activities to extend the traditional course elements of reading, writing, speaking, and listening into translation, pronunciation, class participation, and integration.

Table 2.1 Comparison of Previous and Redesigned Goals

Previous Course Goals	Redesigned Course Goals
Foundational knowledge Memorize vocabulary relating to introductions. Memorize vocabulary relating to school items. Memorize verbs in the present tense.	Foundational knowledge Make introductions, and carry on a conversation in Spanish with a classmate. Use vocabulary relating to school items to describe what you have in your backpack. Use present-tense verbs in conversation.
Application Identify verb tenses. Write an essay introducing two friends. Choose vocabulary relating to food.	Application Use verb tenses to write a Spanish essay. Introduce yourself to a native speaker. Order in Spanish at a Mexican restaurant.
Integration Read about Hispanic culture.	Integration Present an independent study project on Hispanic culture to the class. Human dimension Describe the challenges Hispanic students in our community face. Attend a campus meeting of the Latin American Student Association. Caring Plan a trip to a destination in Latin America. Tell the class about your favorite Mexican holiday. Learning how to learn Make a plan for continued language learning beyond this class. Apply learning skills gained in this class to your learning in other areas.

Translation

Every class session began with translating a new *dicho,* or Spanish proverb. These idiomatic sayings are widely used in the Spanish-speaking world and demonstrate the challenges of translating accurately between English and Spanish.

Each week the students chose one page of Spanish text from a selection of cultural themes to translate into English. They then presented these translations aloud to the class, followed by questions and comments from the group. This activity required the application of foundational knowledge in a new context each week without providing any answers from the back of the text. As the semester progressed I observed the students meeting together before class to check their translations and compare notes. Without realizing it, they were benefiting from each other's experiences and working as a group to improve their translation skills.

NEW DIRECTIONS FOR TEACHING AND LEARNING • DOI: 10.1002/tl

Pronunciation

The fear of speaking in front of others, especially in the target language, often keeps second-language learners from attempting to use their new language skills. Reading aloud in Spanish from a humorous short story during every class helped the students overcome this hesitation and become more comfortable in speaking Spanish.

Class Participation

To involve the students more actively in their learning process, I asked one student to take the lead for each chapter of the textbook. The lead student chose up to thirty (from approximately fifty) vocabulary items presented in each chapter, selected comprehension questions for the class to answer, and led the discussion. The amount of memory work required in the traditional second-year Spanish class can be overwhelming, and I found that students retained more over the course of the semester by focusing on fewer vocabulary words but with more exercises in interaction and application. Involving the students as leaders kept their interest and motivation level high.

Integration

The most significant departure from the traditional class was my requirement that each student complete a capstone project. This project provided integration of the written and spoken course elements and extended student learning into the human dimension, caring, and learning how to learn. Each project consisted of a written essay in Spanish on a topic of the student's choice and an oral presentation or demonstration given to the class. Project topics varied widely. Some students reported on Mexican history and holidays; others translated literature, television shows, and even popular music into Spanish. One wrote and illustrated a short storybook in Spanish, and another demonstrated making a piñata. I was surprised to learn from student evaluations that giving the presentation in front of the class was as much a learning experience for the student as the actual topic studied; I was pleased to see them rise to this challenge and overcome their inhibitions about speaking in front of their peers. As they took turns presenting, the students expressed admiration for the accomplishments of their classmates and began to see themselves as a learning team.

Feedback and Assessment

Fink's illustration (2003) comparing assessment to the scoreboard during a basketball game reshaped my picture of course evaluation. In the traditional class, evaluation consisted of four textbook exams per semester. Like the basketball player who sees his shot go through the net, I wanted my students to have more regular feedback for their work.

During class, we checked homework assignments, short weekly quizzes in grammar, verb worksheets, and translation pieces. This kept the students sharp on their foundational knowledge and built confidence as the course progressed by addressing questions and problems as they arose.

A two-part essay exam at the end of the semester provided a more formal evaluation of integration and application. Half of this exam consisted of a paragraph for the students to translate from Spanish into English. The second half was a two-page essay in Spanish. The students were given clear grading rubrics for both parts of this exam.

Standard letter grades do not accurately reflect the student learning that took place in this class. Each of my students had completed the beginning Spanish class with me at an A level during the previous year. To report that all students earned an A in this class tells little. In the traditional class, earning an A meant that a great deal of student effort went toward memorizing grammar forms and vocabulary specific to the test. They would forget much of this memorization while preparing for the next test and so on throughout the semester. In view of this, I chose to use the textbook exams as take-home tests rather than timed tests in class. This still required the students to learn the foundational grammar material, but allowed them to focus on the reading and writing portions of the test, which I deemed better indicators of overall achievement. I gave these tests four times per semester. In the standard course, text exams accounted for 80 percent of the student grade. My new design divided the course grade evenly among text exams, homework assignments, translation pieces, class participation, and capstone projects.

Student self-evaluation was important throughout the course. From the planning stages through to the final course evaluation, I asked for feedback concerning goals, methods, materials, and activities. For some students, this was the first time they had been asked to consider their own learning goals and was an important step in learning how to learn.

Resources

In addition to the textbook used in the traditional class, I selected a Spanish reader for pronunciation and translation. The students chose a new grammar workbook and used online grammar exercises from a variety of Web sites for reinforcement. A Spanish-language video series provided listening practice and introduced the class to the variety of language use across the Hispanic world.

Course Structure and Teaching Strategy

Weekly class meetings followed a consistent format: introductory conversation (fifteen minutes), grammar and vocabulary exercises (twenty-five minutes), reading and translation in cultural topics (twenty minutes), reading aloud from the Spanish story (thirty-five minutes), and a video presentation (forty minutes). The variety of activities kept class meetings lively and allowed a range of student responses across reading, writing, speaking, and listening skills.

Integrated Learning Activities

Each in-class learning activity was paired with an out-of-class assignment. Grammar lessons were followed by worksheets, and translation exercises introduced in class were completed at home. Readings from the short story were previewed at home before class. Students met before and after class to discuss their capstone projects, which they presented to the group at the end of the term.

Results

Student enthusiasm for this course was strong from the beginning. I was fortunate to have a highly motivated group, ready to try new ideas and willing to expend the effort to complete the independent study required.

Did we meet the goals I set for the course? Absolutely, yes. The primary goal from the beginning was a more active use of Spanish. Throughout the term, students reported finding practical ways to use their growing language skills in conversing with native Spanish speakers at their jobs and in the community. For example, a student employed in a hotel was able to converse with native Spanish-speaking coworkers, while another, employed in a pharmacy, was able to assist Spanish-speaking customers. When asked to evaluate the most significant learning experience in the class, each student commented on how much his or her translation skills had increased and how much his or her comprehension of both spoken and written Spanish had improved. The course had brought their Spanish alive.

I was honest with the group about every course goal except one. Knowing that some students had negative attitudes toward group learning in other classes, I said nothing about my desire for them to work as a learning team. Instead of assigning study groups, I set up learning activities for which there were no clear and easy answers. This forced the students to turn to each other for help with translations and capstone projects. The resulting change in student attitudes toward the value of their peers as learning partners was perhaps the biggest success of all.

Conclusion

Daring to dream up something new, as Fink proposed, meant redesigning the course goals, implementing more active learning activities, and approaching the course from a learning-centered perspective instead of allowing course content to drive my goals. Expanding my learning goals into the human dimension and caring with capstone projects added depth to the course and extended student learning beyond the classroom. The enthusiastic student response to the learning activities and the marked increase in student confidence in using Spanish were clear indicators of course success.

The students in the restaurant speak hesitantly at first, but as the waitress nods and takes their orders without resorting to English, their confidence grows and they relax, pleased to have put their Spanish to use. As the meal concludes, the owner of the restaurant appears and addresses the group. Speaking only in Spanish, he gestures toward an illustrated map of Mexico on the wall and describes the regional specialties of his country. The students listen carefully and smile as the enthusiastic speaker makes a joke in Spanish. He concludes with praise for the effort the group has made in learning about his language and his culture. When he returns to the kitchen, the students congratulate themselves, delighted to have passed the test.

For the students, passing the final exam in the restaurant proved to be more satisfying than any grade I could give and showed the new course design to be successful in applying the classroom foundations of Spanish in a real-world context. ¡Olé!

Reference

Fink, L. D. *Creating Significant Learning Experiences: An Integrated Approach to Designing College Courses.* San Francisco: Jossey-Bass, 2003.

DEBRA DIMON DAVIS *is an adjunct faculty instructor in Spanish at Sauk Valley Community College in Dixon, Illinois. E-mail: davisd@svcc.edu.*

NEW DIRECTIONS FOR TEACHING AND LEARNING • DOI: 10.1002/tl

By using Fink's taxonomy to shape new learning goals and creating new learning and assessment activities, two teachers succeeded in raising students' awareness of the value of their courses and enabled them to become more reflective learners in the process.

More Significant and Intentional Learning in the Economics Classroom

Laurence Miners, Kathryn Nantz

I defined learning in terms of change. For learning to occur, there has to be some kind of change in the learner. No change, no learning. And significant learning requires that there be some kind of lasting change that is important in terms of the learner's life.
L. D. Fink (2003)

Several weeks into the semester, a student arrived a few minutes early for my (Professor Miners) introductory macroeconomics class. She was a strong student and had taken introductory microeconomics with me the previous semester. I asked her how she thought the course was going, and she smiled and said she liked the course better "the old way." "The old way" basically meant more sage-on-the-stage and less guide-on-the-side type of class activities. Although we had been working to redesign our year-long, micro-macro introductory course sequence for several years, clearly we were still missing a piece of the pedagogical puzzle. It was becoming apparent that if we wanted learning to occur, we were going to have to make some changes.

We are grateful for support from the Davis Educational Foundation, established by Stanton and Elizabeth Davis.

NEW DIRECTIONS FOR TEACHING AND LEARNING, no. 119, Fall 2009 © Wiley Periodicals, Inc.
Published online in Wiley InterScience (www.interscience.wiley.com) • DOI: 10.1002/tl.361

Background

We are both teachers in the Economics Department at Fairfield University, a small, comprehensive institution, where we share responsibility for the two courses discussed in this chapter. Our economics students are, for the most part, relatively well prepared and intellectually ready to do the work we assign. However, as the student's comment illustrates, we were apparently not reaching our students in ways that achieved our goals: developing students' abilities to understand economic concepts and apply them to complicated questions regarding resource allocation that they really care about.

At this point, we had designed what we thought were interesting and engaging activities for our students, developed a series of short lectures that were interspersed with group work, and integrated a weekly lab into the course. However, we still were not engaging students in the course material. For example, assignments that we thought would be fun were met with student disinterest. Activities that involved finding data and information on the Web, as well as creating spreadsheets with Excel—the kinds of things we were sure our millennial students would love—were not generating intense student engagement. Why were these strategies not working? Why were student learning outcomes not improving? Why did students appear to prefer more passive approaches to learning?

In addition to this lack of engagement, a common complaint among our economics students had to do with their apparent inability to assess their own progress in the course. Comments like "I knew the material but I couldn't do the problems on the test" or "I understood the problems you worked in class but the ones on the test were harder" indicated that students were not able to assess their own abilities to tackle new and unfamiliar problems or apply the basic concepts under new and different conditions.

Over the same time period, we were working to start a new teaching and learning center at Fairfield. As part of that initiative, we brought Dee Fink to our campus as a consultant and workshop facilitator. After participating in his workshop, which introduced us to the taxonomy of significant learning, it became clear to us that our problem was not the assignments but rather a failure to position our activities in a larger context that would help students appreciate their relevance. Though we had come up with neat, current applications and methodologies, we had not considered the significance of the course as a whole to the students. We had to make the course important in terms of these learners' lives. We had to help them care about the course.

In this chapter, we describe our experience using Fink's taxonomy and course design model to create what we believe are now significant learning experiences for students in our introductory and intermediate economics courses. We describe the changes we made and then discuss what we have found to be positive assessment results from the courses.

NEW DIRECTIONS FOR TEACHING AND LEARNING • DOI: 10.1002/tl

What We Changed

The pedagogical changes that we made fall into two categories. First, we became more intentional in our teaching, incorporating the broad outcomes into our syllabi and making these explicit to students. Second, we provided students with greater opportunities to engage with and internalize the material in new and, we hoped, more interesting ways. In short, we asked them to become reflective learners: those who engage in dimensions of learning that combine cognitive abilities with more affective ones. This combination, we believe, is required to generate the change in a student's perspective that makes significant learning outcomes possible.

Learning Goals

We realized that if we wanted learning outcomes to change, we had to change as well. We used Fink's taxonomy to identify goals for our courses and put them front and center on our syllabi. More important, we went over these goals with the students and, throughout the semester, made an effort to link class activities and assignments back to these goals. We view this step as critically important in our attempt to get students to reflect on their own learning and progress throughout the course.

In both our introductory and intermediate microeconomics courses, we formulated goals based on Fink's taxonomy. The content of these two courses is very similar, but the methods and level of analysis are significantly more complex in the intermediate course. Table 3.1 describes the goals for each course.

We tried to be as transparent as possible with each learning activity. We took care to explain the connection between an activity and our goals, informed students of our expectations, and shared our scoring rubrics when appropriate. We assumed that students would be more likely to do what we asked and partner with us as co-investigators in the course if we clearly enunciated our goals and expectations.

Learning About Our Students

On the first day of the semester, we administered a learning styles survey (Morrison-Shetlar and Marwitz, 2001) to gather additional information about the situational factors that would shape the course. In this survey, students self-identify themselves as auditory, visual, or kinesthetic learners. Although the results are not scientific, we found noteworthy that only one or two students in a typical thirty-student section of introductory microeconomics classified themselves as pure auditory learners. We used this as an opportunity to point out to students that their self-reported preferred learning style was something other than sitting in their seats and listening to us lecture.

Given the considerable variation in scores on this instrument, we took care to develop activities that appealed to our students' diverse learning styles and to help students use the information from their profiles to improve their learning outcomes.

New Directions for Teaching and Learning • DOI: 10.1002/tl

Table 3.1 Specific Learning Goals for Two Courses in Economics

General Type of Significant Learning	Goals for Introduction to Microeconomics	Goals for Intermediate Microeconomics
Foundational knowledge	Remember and be able to use economic terminology. Recall the important functions that government performs in a market economy.	Build your repertoire of economic terms and concepts, and use them appropriately. Understand and use basic algebra and calculus techniques.
Application	Use economic models to understand and explain economic events. Set up and use an Excel worksheet to analyze economic data.	Calculate solutions to calculus-based optimization problems. Analyze the impact of government policies on market outcomes. Solve for optimal levels of output and price for firms operating in alternative market structures.
Integration	Identify the social and political consequences of economic events. Explain the relationships among individuals, firms, and government.	Identify the interaction between economic outcomes in the real world and our abstract theoretical models. Form your own opinions about economies and economic outcomes around the world based on economic theory.
Human dimension	Give examples of how someone's view of economic programs may be influenced by his or her social or economic position. Perceive yourself as a valuable contributor to a team.	Build confidence in your technical skills. Explain economic concepts to classmates and to others, verbally and in writing.
Caring	Have an opinion on economic issues. Be interested in studying the impact of economic programs on different socioeconomic groups.	Identify the usefulness of economic reasoning in personal decision making. Interpret economic current events using the models and theory developed in class.
Learning how to learn	Know how to use all available information in the construction of knowledge. Be aware of and adapt to your individual learning style.	Reflect on your own progress as an economist. Create a learning plan that allows you to think about how you can study and work more efficiently toward your goals in the course.

Throughout the semester, we reminded students of their learning style preferences and suggested strategies they might use outside class to master course concepts. For example, we suggested that auditory learners read the text out loud or explain difficult concepts to one another and that kinesthetic learners stand at a whiteboard to work problems while walking or pacing back and forth. Students reported that they found these strategies helpful to their learning and had never thought about such preferences before.

Teaching and Learning Activities

We developed some common types of activities designed to get students working on all levels of the Fink taxonomy. For example, we used Immediate Feedback Assessment Technique (IF-AT) forms to incorporate Human dimension and real-world Application learning. (This form is a copyrighted instrument that gives students, or more often small groups, immediate feedback, question by question, on how well they are answering questions on a quiz. For more information, see www.epsteineducation.com.) In-class quizzes were completed twice: once individually and a second time as part of a team. The IF-AT form, used by the teams after the individual quizzes are turned in, requires students to discuss and agree on a right answer and then scratch off their selected choice. The correct answer is indicated by an asterisk on the form. If the team gets a wrong answer, they need to discuss again and then scratch off another letter until they get the correct response. Team scores were, on average, 10 to 20 percent higher than even the best individual grades.

We found several important advantages to the IF-AT approach. Within each team, the students became actively engaged in discussing the material and learned from each other. We did not need to go over the correct answers, since the students had already discovered all the correct responses themselves. Rather, we could spend time explaining the few questions that gave several teams some difficulty. These results indicate that this application of the human dimension improved student understanding of the economic concepts.

In addition, we had students design brochures on policy issues (like minimum wages and the North American Free Trade Agreement) to combine integration with caring. These types of authentic assignments asked students to do the kind of work economists do in the real world, combining knowledge of economic concepts with applications that are important to decision making.

In another case, introductory students designed posters focusing on a current economic problem, such as noise pollution, price ceilings, and gasoline prices. We emphasized that there was no prescribed right or wrong government policy intervention but that their policy proposal should be justified on economic grounds and should be consistent with their analysis of the market in question. Students were asked to prepare their posters as if a town meeting was going to be held and their poster would add critical information to the debate. (Perhaps our directions were a little too explicit; a few students asked when the meeting was going to be held.)

Learning How to Learn

Finally, we introduced a series of reflective writing assignments in these courses to help students self-assess where they were with their learning. After exams, students completed a form that asked them to think about how and how much they had studied and which study habits they thought were most and least helpful to their performance. Students were asked at the start of the semester about their understanding and use of economic concepts, and then at the end of the classes about how they perceived the role of government in the economy differently now than they did at the start of the semester.

In another reflective exercise in the introductory course, we asked students to spend time thinking about what they had learned and how their thinking had changed. We used Brookfield's work (1995) as a model to provide students with a structure for their writing and suggested that they reply to some, or all, of the following prompts, though we left the exact format of their writing open to them:

- What have I learned this week about myself as a learner?
- What were the best moments in my learning activities this week?
- What were the worst or most difficult?
- What learning tasks did I respond to most easily?
- What were the most difficult?
- What was the most significant thing that happened to me as a learner this week?
- What learning activity took me by surprise this week?

We encouraged students to complete this exercise weekly and collected their responses at various times during the semester. The following response is illustrative of students in the introductory microeconomics class: "I've learned that just reading out of the book does not help me. I read the text, but I also need someone to discuss it with me and go over things for me to fully understand. I like when I'm given the chance to do things hands on, such as the labs and the group activities because it really makes me work to grasp the concept." Students also wrote about learning experiences that were difficult: "Another difficult activity was the exercise where we split into groups and had to explain the demand curve. This is the area I had not studied before. . . . I got to my group, and the other members were unsure of what to do. I had to step up and be a leader."

In sum, all of the exercises described earlier helped focus student attention on the human dimension, caring, and learning-how-to-learn pieces of the taxonomy, the very pieces that we found absent from our syllabi and course work after attending Fink's seminar. Our next step was to assess these innovations. Did they really contribute to more and better learning?

The Impact of the New Course Design

The combination of developing more authentic assignments and asking students to reflect on their learning resulted in greater student learning and ownership of the material. We received the following reflections after students in intermediate microeconomics had created brochures explaining monopoly pricing at Wal-Mart:

> The reason this issue caught my attention is because this . . . class has completely changed my perspective on companies like Wal-Mart. . . . You start realizing that all issues [like Wal-Mart's monopoly power] have several different players and stakeholders. The key is to focus on all vantage points of a matter; tackle an issue on all possible ends and weigh out the costs and benefits. Also, it is important to recognize what is best for society, not the individual, and what is best in the long run.

Another student wrote:

> The issue that has changed me more than any other in this class was that of Wal-Mart. When we watched the *Frontline* episode [on TV] that asked the question about whether Wal-Mart was good for America . . . I formed some very strong opinions on this subject. For me, it raised the issue of ethics and morality and their role in economic efficiency.

These comments indicate that students were experiencing the change that is fundamental to Fink's paradigm of learning. They were not necessarily changing to be like the teacher, but were aware that their own ideas and thought processes were evolving in fundamental ways.

Not all students liked these "create" exercises, but some really enjoyed the opportunity to construct their own interpretations of their learning. We found that in some cases, students who had difficulty completing the exam questions were good at creating policy analysis posters and brochures. This was a good way to reinforce student confidence for those who were not as good at taking exams. In addition, this technique had potential for actually improving student exam-taking skills by providing assignments that rewarded different learning styles.

Learning How to Learn

Responses after exams indicated that students were thinking carefully about their study habits. One student commented, "I studied all word problems which was probably a bad idea because I more or less memorized those problems and did not know the information." Another said, "I just have to keep calm. Just because something isn't in the format which I'm used to doesn't mean I *can't* do it."

The intentional nature of this writing exercise asks students to take the time to think through their performance and make a plan for improvement. Another student wrote, "I also have to talk out problems with other people, which I did this time . . . talk out problems more often and earlier on." Still another concluded, "On the next test, I'm going to go through problems with a clock so I learn to be more efficient."

Having students become "meta-learners," that is, stepping outside themselves and considering their own learning processes, by using the reflection exercises and their reactions to individual assignments, gave us a greater understanding of what they were taking away from the course. One could argue perhaps that students always had this understanding, and we just did not know it. However, we suspect that completing the exercises also gave them a greater sense of and appreciation for what they learned and how far they came from beginning to end of the semester. This statement from an intermediate microeconomics student illustrates the point:

> The issue this semester that changed my previous thoughts more than any other is price discrimination. . . . Now I understand why firms choose to charge different prices, and the effects that this has on consumers. . . . I guess I have mixed feelings at this point on price discrimination, just because at times it actually helps me. For example, there have been numerous times that I have shown my school ID, and paid a lower price. . . . Other times I am not a fan of price discrimination. When I went to purchase my first car, it was obvious that the price could be negotiated, and as a young teenage girl with her mother I knew they would try to get us to pay a higher price.

Lessons Learned

Being transparent about our teaching goals and making clear connections between those goals and our activities and assignments increased student buy-in to what we were trying to do. When students understood why we were doing particular sorts of exercises and activities, they responded by engaging in them more actively. Because students have different learning styles, it is important to provide them with a variety of ways to connect to course material that is new, technical, and abstract. They appreciated our interest in their learning and our attempts to engage them in different ways and at different levels in conversations about their learning. Finally, we realized that we had to take Fink's quote to heart. We had to change, too: "No change, no learning!" If we were not willing to explore changes in our own teaching methods, we would stop learning about our own courses and students.

References

Brookfield, S. *Becoming a Critically Reflective Teacher*. San Francisco: Jossey-Bass, 1995.
Fink, L. D. *Creating Significant Learning Experiences: An Integrated Approach to Designing College Courses*. San Francisco: Jossey-Bass, 2003.
Morrison-Shetlar, A., and Marwitz, M. *Teaching Creatively: Ideas in Action*. Eden Prairie, Minn.: Outernet Publishing, 2001.

LAURENCE MINERS is director of the Center for Academic Excellence and associate professor of economics at Fairfield University in Connecticut. E-mail: miners@mail.fairfield.edu.

KATHRYN NANTZ is associate professor of economics at Fairfield University. E-mail: nantz@mail.fairfield.edu.

Fink's integrated course design provides a way to put hopeful theory into the reality of practice. The author describes how this model helped him use more active learning experiences that not only deepened students' understanding of musical forms but also enabled students to creatively play with those forms.

Inspiration and Intellect: Significant Learning in Musical Forms and Analysis

Bruce C. Kelley

In his book *Creating Significant Learning Experiences* (2003), Dee Fink challenges professors to create a deep vision for the courses they teach. We as educators often have a vision for what our courses could be, but often lack a model for instituting change. Fink's book provides that model.

I taught the course described in this chapter in 2007–2008 at Shepherd University. Musical Forms and Analysis, the culminating course in music theory for undergraduate music majors at the university, is in many ways the most rewarding course I have taught. After semesters of working through fundamental concepts in theory, such as basic notation and harmonic constructs, students are finally ready to apply their knowledge to much deeper contexts. Their burgeoning musical prowess can now be matched with a similar intellectual rigor.

Rogers (2000, p. 110) writes that one of the challenges of teaching music theory is that "students often lack a basic 'musical horse sense,' through what I [Rogers] call a deficiency of constructive aural brainwashing—not enough soaking in the sonorous nature of the art." Fink's taxonomy provides a vehicle by which we can design our classes to give students significant learning experiences—a soaking in the sonorous nature of our art and a way to make inspiration and intellect not just compatible but positively harmonious. As Madsen (2000, p. 86), states:

NEW DIRECTIONS FOR TEACHING AND LEARNING, no. 119, Fall 2009 © Wiley Periodicals, Inc.
Published online in Wiley InterScience (www.interscience.wiley.com) • DOI: 10.1002/tl.362

We need to develop a core of experiences that represents the best of that which we are capable. The learning from this core should be aimed at establishing in each student the ability to develop his/her basic musicianship as well as to develop a true global music understanding. This core should include a defined knowledge base as well as the ability to analyze, criticize, and choose alternatives based on a compelling personal musical value system.

Fink's integrated course design addresses and builds on these concerns, providing a practical way of putting hopeful theory into the reality of practice.

Redesigning My Class

My introduction to Fink's work began in 2003 when I was awarded a faculty fellowship that allowed me to attend a number of seminars on teaching. The seminars included a week-long workshop on course design that featured creating significant learning experiences. During this workshop, I chose to redesign the culminating course in our music theory sequence, "Forms and Analysis." My goal was to find ways to specifically design Fink's categories of significant learning into the course. What would I want my students to remember five years down the road? What changes (remembering Fink's definition of significant learning as that which causes change in the learners themselves) could I affect in my students' lives through this class?

Learning Goals

I reframed the questions on "what students will be able to do" as learning goals for each of Fink's categories of significant learning. To do this, I used the standard preface for writing learning goals: "My hope is that, by the end of this course, students will . . . ."

Foundational Knowledge
- Be able to model the main musical forms and have a working knowledge of the specialized terms used in describing musical form.
- Understand the concepts and terminology of advanced analytical techniques, such as those used in Schenkerian, feminist, and semiotic analysis.

Application
- Be able to make informed, logical decisions about the formal structure of pieces they are conducting or performing.
- Be able to analyze music in a variety of ways to solve practical problems (for example, score errors) and develop a deeper understanding of the intricacies of the music they are working with.
- Be able to use their understanding of form to improve their composition skills.

Integration
- Be able to understand the significance of formal structures in the pieces they are conducting or performing.
- Be able to see how the study of musical form is linked to fields as diverse as astronomy and literary criticism.

Human Dimension
- See themselves as experts in examining formal processes in music, and develop the confidence to use the skills and techniques they have attained in this class to improve their own musical performances and compositions.
- Develop confidence in their ability to read and understand professional literature in their field.

Caring
- Value the tremendously varied intricacies inherent in musical form and see that music can have multiple meanings. Students will learn to examine music from several different points of view and take time to understand the form of pieces they are conducting or performing.
- Be more attentive to how music is used by society to promote cultural codes.

Learning How to Learn
- Be able to read and understand complex articles dealing with musical analysis.
- Identify some of the more significant resources in the area of musical analysis and learn how to ask useful questions about music they do not understand.

As I defined these learning goals, I simultaneously developed strategies for measuring student progress toward them and devised corresponding sets of teaching and learning activities that created opportunities for students to meet my learning objectives. With this, the initial phase of Fink's integrated course design was finished. (For a more in-depth examination of this sequence and the whole course, see Kelley, 2006.)

The "Pretty Polly" Exercise

One of the several great strengths of Fink's paradigm is that it creates the opportunity to make authentic, meaningful changes within a course. I have always intuitively wanted my students to experience the types of significant learning Fink identified, but before reading his work, I lacked the design structure needed to turn that intuition into deliberately organized learning opportunities.

That structure is provided in the intermediate stage of the integrated approach to course design, where the components of the primary phase are assembled or integrated into a "powerful, dynamic whole" (Fink, 2003, p. 127). Moving back and forth between these intermediate steps of creating a course structure, selecting an effective teaching strategy, and creating the overall scheme of learning activities provides a process for carefully designing opportunities for significant learning.

One series of events from my redesigned course serves particularly well as an example for how the course as a whole was modified and how new activities and ideas were integrated within the more traditional elements of the curriculum. The purpose of this project was to deepen students' ability to analyze the technical characteristics of song form, interpret the meaning of song texts from the perspective of feminist criticism, and use both skills to modify and create new musical forms.

The Class

I was teaching a standard course that met three times a week for fifty minutes with twenty students. Like most other courses on forms and analysis, I planned to spend some time focusing on the basic structures that composers use when writing songs. What I am describing here is a three-day sequence of activities that occurred around the fifth week of the semester. For clarity, I refer to these three days as day 1, day 2, and day 3. This sequence of activities culminated in the "Pretty Polly" project, an assignment that combined written analysis with a musical arrangement.

The events that led up to the "Pretty Polly" project were designed to give students a foundational understanding of the compositional architecture usually associated with songs. But more than that, they were designed to give students the opportunity to interact with these songs through all of the types of significant learning found in Fink's paradigm, which I indicate in brackets.

Prior to Day 1: Two Reading Assignments

Prior to day 1, students were given two reading assignments. The first was from the course textbook on song forms and analyses of songs by the nineteenth-century German composer Franz Schubert [foundational knowledge]. Reading assignments such as this were assessed throughout the course with short quizzes graded by the students themselves in class [learning how to learn]. Recordings of the songs in the textbook were available on departmental listening stations, and my expectation was that students would read the text and listen to the examples prior to class [foundational knowledge].

Students were also expected to read a second assignment, a challenging chapter on feminist literary analysis from Leitch's *American Literary Criticism from the 30s to the 80s* (1988) [integration]. The chapter presents a cogent explanation of the history of feminist criticism and of the myriad (and sometimes contradictory) directions it has taken. I provided a reading guide to help the students navigate through the organization and terminology of the text, and encouraged them to begin reading this a week prior to the first day of the sequence [learning how to learn].

Day 1: Class and an Assignment

During the first half of this period, we analyzed several contemporary songs. I have long endeavored to bring contemporary music into my music theory courses, and the redesign of Forms and Analysis provided the opportunity to incorporate in-class analysis of several popular songs, which still typically use the song form prototypes described in the textbook [application, human dimension]. Songs such as "Six Days on the Road" (written by Earl Green and Carl Montgomery, performed by Sawyer Brown), Ray Charles's "I've Got a Woman," and Carole King's "I Feel the Earth Move" allowed me to add diversity to the course content in terms of composer race, gender, and musical style [human dimension, integration]. King's song, which we analyzed last, stretches the students, for it falls somewhere between the prototype forms, and students are forced (using a variant on the think/pair/share activity) to grapple with the messiness that often typifies real musical form [application].

During the second half of the period, the class discussed the philosophical tenets of feminist analysis (the most controversial topic in the class) and how the array of analytical techniques generated out of feminist philosophy can be used to examine music from new perspectives [foundational knowledge, integration]. The last activity on day 1 required the students to watch a DVD (lang, 1991) of k. d. lang singing her version of "Johnny Get Angry," which would play an important role on day 2 [caring].

Homework Assignment: The assignment was to read an example of feminist scholarship in music: Burns's (1997) "'Joanie' Get Angry: k. d. lang's Feminist Revision" [integration]. This essay examines how lang's remake of the popular 1950s bubblegum pop tune emphasized the implicit violence in the lyrics. Lang achieved this emphasis not only through actions on the stage, but through musical decisions regarding chord substitutions, suspended meter, and orchestration. Students were given a reading guide to help them understand the structure and arguments of the essay [learning how to learn].

Day 2: Class and an Assignment

Most of this day consisted of a continuation of the group discussion on feminism as we examined further what it meant to create a feminist analysis, how Burns's article reflected the major tenets of feminist scholarship as defined by Leitch, and how these tenets were applied to her analysis [foundational knowledge, integration, human dimension].

The class spent the last five minutes of day 2 watching another DVD performance—this time the bluegrass standard "Pretty Polly," as performed by Ralph Stanley and Patty Lovelace on PBS's *All Star Bluegrass Celebration.*

Homework Assignment: After watching this performance, students were asked to write a short essay (due day 3) that examined the disconnect between the lyrics of the text, which describe the murder of a young woman by her lover, and the upbeat, playful performance by Stanley and Lovelace, which stands in direct contrast to lang's performance on "Johnny." This assignment essentially required the students to engage in their own rudimentary feminist critique [application, integration].

Day 3: Class and a Group Performance Assignment
In this session, we began by reviewing the material covered during the preceding week or so, including the song forms [foundational knowledge]. Students were encouraged to ask questions or seek clarification if needed for the essay project described [learning how to learn]. The final portion of the period prepared students for a culminating group performance project.

Assignment: Students were to work in groups of three or four and take the analysis in their short essays one step further by creating their own performance of "Pretty Polly." The specific instructions were as follows:

> Pretty Polly Project: How would *you* change the performance of Pretty Polly to reflect a more direct relationship to the lyrics? Decide in your groups how you might change the instrumentation, fundamental elements such as chord progressions or rhythms, or the performance itself. Although you do not have to perform your entire version (kudos if you can!), I do expect you to be able to provide musical and performance examples of your changes.

Performance: Each group gave their performance of "Pretty Polly" two weeks or so later during the class after the midterm exam. This gave them time to work on their arrangements and put purpose to a day when in the past I had seen reduced attendance. Their performance was graded with a rubric emphasizing creativity and analytical insight.

Conclusion

So what effect did these changes have? Prior to my redesign, discussion of song forms would have ended on the second day, and the class would have been off to the next model form. My redesign gave students the chance to think more deeply about the special relationship of music, text, and performance in ways that encouraged significant learning. This project quickly became one of the favorites of the class. Student performances reset "Pretty Polly" in styles as diverse as smooth jazz, Beatle-influenced rock, heavy metal, and Broadway. The performances became so popular that students outside the course, especially those who had already taken Forms and had done the project, asked to sit in on the class to hear this year's groups play and explain their compositional decisions.

One student wrote on a course evaluation, "I think doing more projects like the Pretty Polly project would give a better hands-on understanding of the course material." Another added, "The inclusion of the group project enabled us to put theory into application, which was very helpful." As a whole, the series of projects leading up to the group performance of "Pretty

Polly" moved students far beyond foundational knowledge and made significant strides towards achieving my other learning goals.

Fink's *Creating Significant Learning Experiences* provides a highly useful model for course design that is centered on a revolutionary paradigm of significant learning. I believe that it is to our benefit to consider strongly this new approach, for it provides a stimulating model to bring deep, meaningful learning to our courses—an integration at the highest levels of both inspiration and intellect.

References

Burns, L. "'Joanie' Get Angry: k. d. lang's Feminist Revision." In J. Covach and G. M. Boone (eds.), *Understanding Rock: Essays in Musical Analysis.* New York: Oxford University Press, 1997.

Fink, L. D. *Creating Significant Learning Experiences: An Integrated Approach to Designing College Courses.* San Francisco: Jossey-Bass, 2003.

Kelley, B. "Design for Change: Creating Significant Learning Experiences in the Music Classroom." *College Music Symposium*, 2006, 46, 64–76.

lang, k. d. *Harvest of Seven Years.* Burbank, Calif.: Warner Reprise Video, 1991. DVD.

Leitch, V. *American Literary Criticism from the 30s to the 80s.* New York: Columbia University Press, 1988.

Madsen, C. "Music Education: A Future I Would Welcome." *College Music Symposium*, 2000, 40, 84–90.

Rogers, M. "How Much and How Little has Changed? Evolution in Theory Teaching." *College Music Symposium*, 2000, 40, 110–116.

BRUCE C. KELLEY is the founding director of the Center for Teaching and Learning at The University of South Dakota, where he is also an associate professor of music. E-mail: bruce.kelley@usd.edu.

This chapter presents an interdisciplinary approach to course redesign that enhanced student learning across all six categories in Fink's taxonomy. A meta-analysis of the results provides evidence that integrated course design produces significant learning.

Using Fink's Integrated Course Design: How a Book Changed Our Students' Learning, Our University, and Ourselves

Carolyn R. Fallahi, Laura E. Levine, Joan M. Nicoll-Senft, Jack T. Tessier, Cheryl L. Watson, Rebecca M. Wood

In December 2003, while searching for a reading for our university's Center for Teaching Excellence book club, Joan Nicoll-Senft stumbled on Dee Fink's *Creating Significant Learning Experiences* (2003). This chance occurrence began an interdisciplinary collaboration of six faculty members that has grown from a book discussion to a research project to a university-wide program.

In this chapter, we have four connected stories to tell: (1) how Fink's book challenged us to change our teaching in lasting ways; (2) how we used this inspiration to assess Fink's ideas about integrated course design (ICD) empirically in a scholarship of teaching and learning (SoTL) model of research; (3) how our experiences helped to spread these ideas within our university and beyond; and (4) how this whole experience changed us. We hope this chapter inspires other faculty members to apply these ideas to create significant learning experiences for their students and also for themselves.

The Challenge to Ourselves and Our Teaching

In 2002, the Center for Teaching Excellence at our university initiated a book discussion club that meets several times each semester to discuss

NEW DIRECTIONS FOR TEACHING AND LEARNING, no. 119, Fall 2009 © Wiley Periodicals, Inc.
Published online in Wiley InterScience (www.interscience.wiley.com) • DOI: 10.1002/tl.363

books as wide ranging as Parker Palmer's *The Courage to Teach* (1997) and Rebekah Nathan's *My Freshman Year* (2005). In spring 2004, while discussing Fink's *Creating Significant Learning Experiences*, we began to formulate an idea to put his ideas about course design into action. At this point, six interested members of the book club became a SoTL group. Part of the challenge and the interest of this group is that it brought together faculty members from four disciplines: psychology, biology, special education, and biomolecular sciences.

ICD: Moving from Ideas to Application to Research

Each of us had expressed concerns about how well students were learning in one course that we were teaching. We all wanted to make changes to our course, but had never had a structure to help us accomplish these goals. Our tendency was to focus on innovative activities instead of a systematic approach based on the goals we had for our courses.

We were excited about the possibilities that Fink's structure might afford our teaching. Fink's approach to course design emphasizes beginning with the instructor's long-term goals for student learning, an approach called backward design (Fink, 2003). With that in mind, we used Fink's taxonomy of significant learning as a framework for creating the learning goals for our courses: foundational knowledge (FK), application (A), integration (I), human dimension (HD), caring (C), and learning how to learn (LHL). Our basic question was what knowledge, attitudes, and modes of thinking we wanted students to retain long after the course was over. We then created assessments to determine whether students had achieved those goals. Finally, we changed the way we taught our courses in order to achieve those goals.

What We Did

Each of the six professors collaborating in this project followed the same basic process: identify major learning goals, figure out how to assess that learning, and identify the learning activities to promote that kind of learning. However, the individual responses reflected the specific subject matter and context of their courses (Table 5.1).

Carolyn Fallahi: "Lifespan Development"

Carolyn faced two major challenges in teaching this course. First, the course has extensive content. It covers physical, social, emotional, cognitive, and moral development from conception through death. Second, she teaches large sections of the course—often up to two hundred students per section. Her primary change efforts were to move her learning goals beyond foundational knowledge (FK) and achieve more application (A) and integration

(I), and then move beyond lecturing on the material to incorporating more active learning.

In order to assess these goals, she used multiple-choice questions that surveyed course content (FK), essay questions on case studies that examined students' abilities to apply the concepts (A) and provide solutions to practical problems (I), and Likert scale assessments that examined students' level of caring and interest in the course, knowledge about themselves, and knowledge and comfort with research tools used to examine course content (C, LHL).

The new learning activities focused on case studies of neglected and bullied children. The students followed these case studies throughout the semester, and as they were introduced to new concepts, they applied that knowledge to the case studies. By the end of the semester, their understanding of childhood issues and available interventions for those children had grown immensely.

Laura Levine: "The Psychology of Early Childhood"
The major goal in changing this course was to promoting students' ability to learn how to learn (LHL). Laura wanted her students, long after the course was over, to be able to answer questions that would come up about children with whom they interacted. She wanted them to be able to use scientifically based sources of information and evaluate the information they found.

To assess this at the end of the semester, students used a Likert scale to rate their ability to find professional resources. They also demonstrated their knowledge of resources available to help children by finding articles related to specific questions.

To help students become active learners who could find the answers to their own questions about children, she required them to observe and interact with young children. However, instead of making up and assigning specific observations, as she had done in the past, she had them work in groups around computers to create their own observational assignments concerning questions of interest to them. They searched professional databases to find research on their topics of interest to help them develop ways in which to observe children and come to a better understanding of their development.

Joan Nicoll-Senft: "Instructional Planning for Students with Exceptionalities"
Joan was also concerned about her students' ability to be self-directed learners (LHL). As future special education teachers, they would face ongoing challenges pertaining to the education of students with a wide range of disabilities and needed to learn how to problem-solve effectively.

She used Fink's integrated course design approach to incorporate problem-based learning in her course. She developed three scenarios based

Table 5.1 Types of Assessment, by Course

	Lifespan Development	Instructional Planning for Students with Exceptionalities	Concepts in Biology	Psychology of Early Childhood	Anatomy and Physiology I
FK	Multiple-choice questions pertaining to course content.	Very short-answer, multiple-choice questions and matching to test vocabulary.	Multiple-choice questions pertaining to course content.	Multiple-choice and essay questions pertaining to course content.	Multiple-choice questions pertaining to course content.
A	Student essays on two case studies were scored on knowledge and quality of response.	The purpose of various components of educational planning was identified by students, who also provided examples of each component.	Students wrote an explanation of a news story about biology and an explanation of what information was left out of the story.	Students wrote essay questions applying concepts to children's behavior.	Student wrote essays solving a case study involving human motion.
I	Students generated possible solutions to a case study. Their responses were scored on knowledge and quality of response.	Developed appropriate accommodations or modifications for learning based on a case study.	Students wrote an explanation of the relevance of biology news to other biology topics and the student's own life.	Students used an essay format to interrelate issues in child psychology.	Multiple-choice questions.

C	Likert scale assessment of level of caring and interest regarding topics covered in class.	Students wrote an essay response to an article on equity and excellence in education.	Likert scale assessment of student's opinions about peer interactions.	Likert scale assessment of student's attitudes about young children.	Multiple-choice questions.
HD	Likert scale assessment of new knowledge about self or human beings in general.	Students wrote a brief reflection on personal attributes, strengths, and needs pertaining to collaborating in educational planning.	Likert scale assessment of student's opinions about his or her thoughts and feelings regarding biology topics.	Likert scale assessment of student's confidence in his or her ability to interact with young children.	Multiple-choice questions.
LHL	Students asked where they could get more information on a topic from a magazine. Responses were scored on knowledge and quality of response. Likert scale assessment of comfort level with research tools.	Students wrote statements pertaining to self-directed learning and self-reflection. Likert scale used.	Students wrote explanations of why they did or did not trust the source of biology news and did a presentation of additional sources used to understand the biology news.	Likert scale was used for students to do a self-appraisal of their ability to find needed information, evaluate a news article, write articles on the same topic, and find resources to help children.	Multiple-choice questions.

on challenges she had faced as a teacher, an administrator, and an educational consultant. These three problems became the framework for the course, with students working in small, heterogeneous groups to develop solutions to their scenarios and eventually share their work with their classmates.

To assess her redesign efforts, students used a Likert scale to rate their ability to develop flexible lesson plans based on their interests and learning styles.

Jack Tessier: "Concepts in Biology"

Jack wanted to help students to see the daily importance of biology to their lives (HD, C). He used Fink's approach, in addition to peer teaching (Tessier, 2007), to teach students how to apply the content of the lesson and understand the relevance of a particular concept by linking that concept to current events in biology (Levine and others, forthcoming).

In order to assess these goals, he used two-page news article reports (which assessed all of Fink's taxa of significant learning) and had students do in-class reviews of news articles with each unit covered.

Cheryl Watson: "Anatomy and Physiology I"

Cheryl wanted to help her students develop skills that they would take beyond their final exams and into their real lives. One of her major goals was to increase student retention of the material by impressing on them how essential anatomy and physiology are in their daily lives (FK, I).

She assessed their ability to apply the material by using essay questions on the exam. The lessons were repetitive and additive. In several learning units, she asked them to pick up a cup from the table and to build their understanding by explaining what was happening as they did so, involving first bones, then muscles, then muscle attachments, then nerves.

This simple case study of picking up a cup is arguably the shortest case study in history. However, it is a daily part of our students' lives, and they will see themselves do this task thousands of times in a semester.

Rebecca Wood: "Lifespan Development"

Rebecca had three goals for her section of this course: to promote integration and application of the wide array of topics presented during the course (A, I), inspire caring about the material (C), and help students learn how to learn (LHL).

To evaluate these outcomes, she created a multiformat assessment with multiple-choice, essay, and Likert scale questions. Multiple-choice questions targeted fundamental knowledge, which was expected to improve by the end of the semester but was not the main focus of the course. The essay questions targeted integration and application, and most of these presented a scenario that students had to explain using the course material. For example, one of the questions described an adolescent girl who was rejected by her peers. Students were asked to provide some reasons for the peer rejection and offer some solutions to the problem. The Likert scale items focused on caring and learning how to learn. Some LHL items, for example, asked students to rate their knowledge of various library services.

She incorporated two activities into her course to address these goals. The first was a "design a toy" project. Students were placed into groups and assigned a particular age group (for example, late infancy, middle childhood). Their task was to design an age-appropriate toy, taking into consideration the motor, perceptual, cognitive, and social capabilities of children in their assigned age range. This part of the project was designed to address integration and application of the course material on child development. The project also involved a literature review, which required students to cite empirical evidence that their toys could be used by children of that age. Thus, students had to find and analyze original research articles and apply the information to their projects. This part of the exercise targeted learning-how-to-learn skills.

The second activity involved the other end of the life span and was designed to address the issue of caring. For this activity, she put students through a simulated aging exercise. Students were fitted with surgical gloves filled with popcorn kernels to simulate arthritis, earplugs to create a loss of hearing, beans in their shoes to cause foot discomfort and balance problems, and glasses smeared with Vaseline to impair vision. Students were then asked to perform everyday activities such as making peanut butter sandwiches. They also did a craft project involving peeling the backs off stickers and making a design with them. Students then wrote a paper about their own experience and how their ideas about the challenges elderly people face changed as a result of the activity.

Impact on Student Engagement and Learning

To complete our SoTL project, we conducted a meta-analysis of all of our assessments to determine if, across disciplines, there was significant improvement in student learning and abilities based on the six taxa Fink described. We found the improvements in foundational knowledge, application, the human dimension, and learning how to learn were statistically significant across all four disciplines (see Table 5.2). Although there were improvements in both integration and caring across all six courses, they were not statistically significant.

When we looked more closely at the data on integration and caring, we found a number of interesting observations. First, three of the courses did have an improvement in integration, and one of the six courses had a significant improvement in caring (based on within-course t-tests of pre- and postcourse tests).

One of the statistical problems was the ceiling effect. Students in courses where significant improvement was not found in caring often had

Table 5.2 Meta-Analysis Results Comparing Pre- and Postsemester Means as a Percentage of Available Points Across Fink's Taxonomy

Taxon	Presemester Mean	Postsemester Mean
Foundational knowledge	0.508	0.668[a]
Application	0.400	0.607[a]
Integration	0.503	0.618
Human dimension	0.640	0.740[a]
Caring	0.613	0.683
Learning how to learn	0.520	0.595[a]

[a]Means are significantly different from the presemester mean at $\alpha = 0.05$.

Source: Levine and others (forthcoming).

pretest scores near the ceiling and therefore had a limited potential to increase in their level of caring about the subject. These included students in special education and psychology and students in biomolecular sciences whose major focus was health care. We also found integration to be a particularly difficult taxon to operationalize, and the lack of significant results in the meta-analysis may simply be an artifact of this challenge.

The important lesson from our collective effort to statistically assess student learning in our redesigned courses is this: the approach we used in redesigning our courses was capable of creating measurable improvement in all six categories of Fink's taxonomy.

The Expansion of Our SoTL Efforts

After our group's research was completed, our dissemination efforts began. We pursued many avenues, within and outside our university, to share our findings and experiences. In 2005, we were invited to present a workshop on Fink's approach to course redesign to new and nontenured faculty at our university. This led to a series of consecutive workshops on the same topic, where we were paired with faculty from various disciplines to provide one-on-one mentoring on Fink's approach to course redesign. We also presented our research findings on Fink's approach at a university-sponsored research conference and published our findings in a university-based monograph (Levine and others, 2006).

Outside our university, we gave workshops to present our experiences and introduce others to our application of Fink's ideas and disseminated our collective findings through publications (Levine and others, 2007, 2008). Individual members of our group also published more detailed accounts of their work with Fink's approach to course redesign in discipline-specific journals (Fallahi, 2008; Fallahi and LaMonaca, 2009a; Fallahi and La-Monaca, 2009b; Nicoll-Senft, 2006).

In spring 2007, our university, inspired by the success of our group, decided to initiate SoTL circles: small groups of faculty interested in studying an aspect of teaching, systematically implementing changes in their courses, and assessing the impact of these changes on the teaching and learning process. These groups carried out their work during the 2007–2008 academic year and presented their findings at a university-sponsored colloquium attended by over fifty university faculty and administrators at the culmination of the spring 2008 semester. Although each group focused on differing content to plan their course changes, Fink's ideas about course design have formed the basis for this initiative.

Four Years Later: The Effects on Us

In discussing how our teaching and course design has evolved since we began this project, we all agreed on several points. We now always begin our course design by asking three questions: "What do we want students to retain from this course?" "How can we make this learning personal for the student?" and "How can we make this a human experience that will make them care about the material?" This is a very different approach from asking, "How can I cover the textbook material in one semester?" Clearly each member of our group has experienced a lasting change in his or her approach to course organization.

When we were inspired by Fink's book and informally formed a small group of faculty to implement his ideas about course design in 2004, we were unaware of what was to come of it. We had no idea that we would reach the larger goals of improved student learning, engagement in the scholarship of teaching and learning, and dissemination of these ideas beyond our university. The work that we have engaged in has influenced faculty both inside and outside our university. Fink's ideas about course redesign provide a means for teachers in all disciplines to create more significant learning for their students. We have shown that our students learned and grew in many ways—and at the same time, so did we.

References

Fallahi, C. R. "Redesign of a Life Span Development Course Using Fink's Taxonomy." *Teaching of Psychology,* 2008, 35(3), 169–175.

Fallahi, C. R., & LaMonaca, F. H. "The Evolution of Educational Objectives: Bloom's Taxonomy and Beyond." *Journal on Excellence in College Teaching,* 2009a, 20(1), 71–86.

Fallahi, C. R., and LaMonaca, F. M. "Creating Significant Learning Experiences in a Large Undergraduate Psychology Class: A Pilot Study." *Journal on Excellence in College Teaching,* 2009b, 20(1), 87–100.

Fink, L. D. *Creating Significant Learning Experiences: An Integrated Approach to Designing College Courses.* San Francisco: Jossey-Bass, 2003.

Levine, L., and others. "Creating Significant Learning Experiences Across the Curriculum." In P. Lemma (ed.), *Systematic Reflections on the Scholarship of Teaching Monograph*. New Britain: Central Connecticut State University, Center for Teaching Excellence, 2006.

Levine, L., and others. "Teaching Ourselves: A Model to Improve, Assess and Spread the Word." *International Journal for the Scholarship of Teaching and Learning*, 2007, 1(2). http://www.georgiasouthern.edu/ijSoTL/current.htm.

Levine, L. E., and others. "Creating Significant Learning Experiences Across Disciplines in Higher Education." *College Teaching*, 2008, 56(4), 247–254.

Nathan, R. *My Freshman Year: What a Professor Learned by Becoming a Student*. Ithaca, N.Y.: Cornell University Press, 2005.

Nicoll-Senft, J. "Creating Significant Learning Experiences Across the Curriculum." Paper presented at the Annual Connecticut State University Faculty Research Conference, New Britain, Conn., Oct. 2006.

Palmer, P. J. *The Courage to Teach: Exploring the Inner Landscape of a Teacher's Life*. San Francisco: Jossey-Bass, 1997.

Tessier, J. T. "Small Group Peer Teaching in an Introductory Biology Classroom." *Journal of College Science Teaching*, 2007, 36(4), 64–69.

CAROLYN R. FALLAHI *is an associate professor of psychology at Central Connecticut State University. E-mail: FallahiC@mail.ccsu.edu.*

LAURA E. LEVINE *is an associate professor of psychology at Central Connecticut State University. E-mail: levinel@mail.ccsu.edu.*

JOAN M. NICOLL-SENFT *is an associate professor of special education at Central Connecticut State University. E-mail: nicoll-senftj@ccsu.edu.*

JACK T. TESSIER *is an assistant professor of biology at the State University of New York at Delhi. E-mail: tessiejt@delhi.edu.*

CHERYL L. WATSON *is a professor of biomolecular sciences at Central Connecticut State University. E-mail: watsonc@ccsu.edu.*

REBECCA M. WOOD *is an assistant professor of psychology at Central Connecticut State University. E-mail: woodre@ccsu.edu.*

NEW DIRECTIONS FOR TEACHING AND LEARNING • DOI: 10.1002/tl

A very experienced teacher faces the challenge of teaching a new course where students meet face-to-face only ten times.

Using Integrated Course Design to Build Student Communities of Practice in a Hybrid Course

Harriet R. Fayne

Two years ago, I was approached by a colleague who directs a teacher resource center with an intriguing and challenging request. Would I be willing to design a course that would help special education teachers satisfy the "Highly Qualified Teacher" (HQT) requirement established by No Child Left Behind (NCLB) in the area of English/language arts? Sure, I responded. The time was right. I was scheduled for a sabbatical and wanted to reenter the world of special education in order to update my knowledge and skills. What better way to get to know about the lived experience of special educators than by working closely with them over ten weeks?

After more than thirty years of teaching, I was comfortable, perhaps too comfortable, with the performance aspects of my job. I regularly received high marks on course evaluation items measuring instructor variables (enthusiasm, knowledge of subject matter, explanations, use of real-life examples, and instructional variety). However, I had started to notice an increase in lukewarm ratings on items that tap students' perceptions of their own learning and engagement (critical and independent thinking, effort, creativity, and amount learned). Since I had a chance to develop a new course for practicing teachers, it seemed an opportune time to try out a different planning regimen, one that would help me focus less on my teaching skills and more on student learning outcomes.

NEW DIRECTIONS FOR TEACHING AND LEARNING, no. 119, Fall 2009 © Wiley Periodicals, Inc.
Published online in Wiley InterScience (www.interscience.wiley.com) • DOI: 10.1002/tl.364

The approach I chose was based on principles advanced by Fink in *Creating Significant Learning Experiences: An Integrated Approach to Designing College Courses* (2003). The term *integration* is central to his thesis: significant learning is more likely to occur if there is clear alignment among goals, assessments, and instructional activities; if contextual factors are taken into account; if active strategies that involve experiential learning and reflection are adopted; and if assessments are educative in nature. Since I knew that it would be hard to get to know my students or for students to get to know one another in a class that met only ten times, I consulted *Collaborating Online: Learning Together in Community* (Palloff and Pratt, 2005) for ways to use technology as a vehicle to increase opportunities for interaction and therefore improve the odds that significant learning would occur.

Fink suggests that course design begin with an analysis of situational factors: time allocation, class size, student characteristics, teacher characteristics, and external constraints. To learn more about the twenty-three students who had signed up for the course, I administered an online survey. I must admit that my initial enthusiasm waned a bit after looking at the results. Participants were not excited about the prospect of taking this course. Approximately one-third expressed feelings that ranged from annoyance to outrage; half were simply resigned to jump through the hoops established by state and federal authorities. Regardless of where they landed along the attitude spectrum, the teachers sent me a consistent message: *We are qualified (if evaluated by legitimate versus NCLB criteria), and we resent the fact that arbitrary course requirements, which have little or no relationship to our teaching situations, have been sprung on us.*

I had my work cut out for me. I knew that I had to find a way to build on and celebrate participants' prior knowledge, provide resources that they would deem useful and practical, and create a positive climate that would allow a community of practice to develop across the ten class meetings. If I failed to design a course that led to significant learning for the teachers who had signed up for the course, it was going to be a long ten weeks.

Making Lemonade out of Lemons Takes Careful Planning

Although the Ohio Department of Education did not provide a specific course outline, it was understood that considerable attention was to be given to the Ohio Academic Content Standards in English/Language Arts and standards-based instruction. From that starting point, I used Fink's *Taxonomy of Significant Learning* to structure my thinking. Foundational knowledge goals were easy to articulate, largely because instructional objectives for a teacher educator represent business as usual. The other dimensions (learning how to learn, the human dimension, caring, application, and integration) were more challenging to translate into goals, but Fink's framework reminded me that it was important to do so. I decided to establish one major learning goal per dimension.

The next step was to come up with key assessments that would align with these goals. Since I had determined that it was important for my students to engage with the course material, care deeply about their own professional development as well as that of their colleagues, and think critically and creatively, I wanted to use formative techniques (what Fink calls educative feedback) that would not only inform my decisions but would allow student voices to be heard in the assessment process. Once the goals and feedback procedures were identified, I selected activities that would become teaching-learning routines across the ten weeks. In order to make sure that all of the components complemented one another (in Fink's terms, the goals, assessments, and teaching-learning activities were integrated), I created the three-column chart provided in Table 6.1.

Learning how to learn was of particular importance. The class would last only ten weeks, and I wanted participants to continue to grow professionally long after it was over. Here is where technology played a major role. I set up a course Web site. Across the ten weeks, participants would be asked to locate lesson plans, articles, and materials that could be posted on the Web site so that the entire class could benefit from their research. Finding online resources and determining whether they incorporate best practices is an essential skill for teachers, who can easily become overwhelmed by the plethora of information available on the Internet.

The Role of Student Learning Communities

I hoped to get buy-in by identifying four literacy themes that would serve as organizing structures for the Web site and then dividing the class into small learning communities, with each learning community taking on one theme. These learning communities would also address the goals of the human dimension and caring. Students would choose a community that matched their interests. Groups would be given guiding questions, readings, and a blank log to record minutes and communicate questions or concerns to me. I set aside an hour for community meetings, with ten minutes at the beginning of each meeting devoted to sharing classroom highs and lows from the past week. On a weekly basis, the groups were to assign the following roles to individuals: recorder, materials manager, discussion forum moderator, and timekeeper. Each community had its own online discussion forum; everyone was required to submit at least five postings across the ten weeks. The groups were responsible for a final presentation on their topic that included a listing of Web-based resources.

For the second hour of class each week, I addressed foundational knowledge and application by modeling standards-based teaching strategies. For the large group segment of each class, I had designed minilessons

**Table 6.1 Three-Column Table for Fayne's Hybrid Course:
Highly Qualified Teaching**

Learning Goals	Assessment Activities	Teaching-Learning Activities
Learning how to learn: Students should be able to locate and evaluate Web-based resources that can enhance their teaching practices.	Peer review of online literacy resources	Construction of a course Web site with links to peer-reviewed online resources that demonstrate best literacy practices
Caring: Students should have opportunities to talk about classroom highs and lows.	Interactive logs kept by learning communities (with course instructor responses)	Learning community meetings held for one hour each week across the term (ten minutes set aside for "highs" and "lows")
Human dimension: In order to promote positive interdependence, students should share teaching strategies and resources.	Online discussion forums Final presentation by each learning community with class debriefing	Collaborative learning strategies employed by the learning communities (Johnson, Johnson, and Smith, 1991)
Foundational knowledge: Students should enhance their knowledge of English/ language arts standards and standards-based instruction.	Classroom assessment techniques: Exit slips and one-minute papers (Angelo and Cross, 1993)	Minilessons modeling best practices
Application: Students should try out standards-based instruction in their own classrooms.	Classroom assessment techniques End-of-term survey	Classroom discussion
Integration: Students should link personal and professional literacy skills.	Individual reading/writing conferences	Writing a teaching auto-biography and keeping a reading log

demonstrating ways to embed explicit vocabulary and comprehension instruction in a literature unit (using the assigned young adult novel) as well as developmentally appropriate methods to address common spelling, grammar, and word recognition problems of special needs adolescents. After introducing a strategy, I encouraged participants to put it into practice and report back by sharing their experiences in class or giving me feedback on an exit slip or a one-minute paper (adapted from Angelo and Cross, 1993).

During the last hour of each class, I focused on integration by helping participants to see the connection between personal literacy habits and teaching practices. I held individual reading and writing conferences during which I could provide feedback on drafts of the teaching autobiography

NEW DIRECTIONS FOR TEACHING AND LEARNING • DOI: 10.1002/tl

assignment and, when time permitted, converse about the books the participants had listed on their reading logs. In addition to giving me a wonderful opportunity to know my students as readers and writers, I was hoping to model conferencing as a powerful assessment technique.

Sharing Authority with Students

I posted the first prompt on each group's discussion board: "What do you already know about the topic of—? What are some of your questions and concerns about—?" On the Struggling Readers discussion forum, one participant asked if anyone had any good high-interest, easy-vocabulary materials to recommend. I suggested comic books. Soon after I posted my response, a student politely but clearly weighed in, indicating that she did not agree with my suggestion:

> I have comic books in a container with other children's magazines (National Geographic Kids, Kids Discover, etc) and the comic books are consistently overlooked. I finally asked one of the boys why they don't choose to read the comic books and he said that they were too hard to follow (which square to read first and which bubble to read first). Odd eh? Also, he said that he thought the pictures and captions in the "educational" magazines were cool and he felt like he was learning.

It became apparent very quickly that students as well as the teacher could be authorities in this course. Week after week, the discussion forums expanded, with participants responding to readings, sharing ideas, and asking for suggestions. I found myself scrambling to update the course Web site daily, incorporating links as well as information on other resources mentioned in postings. My role was shifting from sole authority figure and performer to one that allowed students to experience their own agency as learners and facilitate the learning of their peers. The easy give-and-take spilled over to the classroom sessions as well. By the third week of class, participants were bringing curriculum materials, favorite titles, and games to show classmates. One student captured the feeling shared by a number of her colleagues: "I think that it is so refreshing to sit down with other like-minded educators to talk about ideas, frustrations, and successes. There is little time to do this in our day-to-day activities."

But what about the foundational knowledge and the application assignments that the Ohio Department of Education would want to see at the end of a Highly Qualified Teacher course? Although there were no tests used to measure knowledge, one-minute papers and exit slips provided me with sufficient data to conclude that participants were grasping the essentials of standards-based instruction. On the end-of-course survey, students indicated that not only had they acquired knowledge of some powerful teaching strategies but also had been motivated enough to try them out in their own classrooms. Five of the fifteen techniques that had been covered in mini-lessons had been used by over half of the participants and another five by one-third of the group. All fifteen had been employed by at least three individuals.

The course had not been as successful at getting participants to appreciate the connection between personal literacy and teaching as it had been at encouraging participation in a community of practice focused on language arts instruction. Online survey data indicated that a sizable minority (39 percent) would have been happy to eliminate the personal literacy component of the course. The autobiographies and reading logs, as well as the class activities associated with these two course components, were perceived as busywork by some and burdensome academic requirements by others. Their reactions reminded me that teachers are practical-minded students who want ideas they can apply immediately in their work situations. I will not abandon the goal; instead, I will experiment further to find activities and assessments that help teachers to see that their growth as language learners will have a beneficial impact on their students.

Overall, participants were very positive about the course. The lukewarm ratings on engagement and learning items that had troubled me in the past were not evident on the HQT course evaluations. Twenty-two of the twenty-three teachers felt that the course was challenging, nineteen believed that they had been required to think independently and creatively, and twenty concluded that they had learned a great deal. The online postsurvey, administered separately from the standard course evaluation, revealed a shift from the largely neutral (ten participants) or negative (seven participants) attitudes expressed on the presurvey. Students were either extremely positive (nine participants), positive (ten participants), or neutral (four participants) about the course after having taken it.

Lessons Learned

Like my students, I, too, experienced significant learning in the HQT course. By applying Fink's design principles, I learned how to tailor a course to a particular audience. Because I had taken into account the human and caring dimensions, I had empowered and energized students who came in feeling disempowered and unmotivated.

One important lesson learned (or relearned) is how much context matters. Taking into account situational factors such as students' backgrounds and expectations, I asked myself: What are these students motivated to learn? How can I match my course with their needs? The answers to these questions shaped both structure and content. Without careful forethought, it would have been easy to blame external forces or the students if the course headed in a negative direction.

I also learned (and perhaps this really was new learning for me) that what Fink terms "educative feedback" does not come solely from the instructor. I responded to the journals kept by each learning community, posted responses on each discussion forum, and held individual writing conferences. In addition, I kept up e-mail correspondence with anyone in the class who wished to get in touch with me. However, equally powerful (if not more powerful) feedback came from class leaders who emerged across the ten weeks.

In each community, at least one individual, often someone with a wealth of ideas, provided direction and concrete suggestions not only about course requirements but also about ways to resolve teaching dilemmas. There was no way that I could have anticipated who these leaders would be. In the future, I have to have faith that there will be students in all of my classes who will rise to the occasion and play this role. I also have to provide opportunities through the way I design my courses to allow space for these leaders to demonstrate and share their expertise.

Using Fink's integrated approach to course design freed me to grow professionally in my own class. The physical and virtual conversations gave me a view into twenty-three classrooms. I was one teacher among many, and together we were learning how to strengthen the literacy skills of special needs adolescents. Since most of the course preparation was done before the course began, I just had to fine-tune based on my own reflections and participant feedback. Students now had a significant voice, and I was in a position to listen to and act on what they were telling me.

References

Angelo, T. A., and Cross, K. P. *Classroom Assessment Techniques.* San Francisco: Jossey-Bass, 1993.

Fink, L. D. *Creating Significant Learning Experiences: An Integrated Approach to Designing College Courses.* San Francisco: Jossey-Bass, 2003.

Johnson, D. W., Johnson, R. T., and Smith, K. A. *Cooperative Learning: Increasing College Faculty Instructional Productivity.* ASHE-ERIC Higher Education Report No. 4. Washington, D.C.: School of Education and Human Development, George Washington University, 1991.

Palloff, R. M., and Pratt, K. *Collaborating Online: Learning Together in Community.* San Francisco: Jossey-Bass, 2005.

HARRIET R. FAYNE is a professor in the Education Department at Otterbein College, Westerville, Ohio. E-mail: hfayne@otterbein.edu.

Two humanities professors shift from the rut of readings, memorization, and papers to having students ask personalized questions and make concepts relevant outside the classroom.

Integrating Big Questions with Real-World Applications: Gradual Redesign in Philosophy and Art History

Marice Rose, Roben Torosyan

As a philosopher and an art historian, we decided to record our experience after discovering we shared similar journeys changing our courses. We had both been dissatisfied with our students' learning outcomes and our own tired patterns of teaching.

After learning about Fink's (2003) integrated course design (ICD) and his six kinds of learning objectives, we both saw ways to have students not only learn required foundational material but also apply that learning to life, communicate creatively about it, and value the resulting experience deeply. We were ready to change the way we teach. With transformed methods—and some bumps and dead-ends along the way—we envisioned larger dreams; helped our students integrate goals, activities, and assessments; and experienced a sense of continuing renewal in our teaching energies.

This chapter highlights our individual efforts to transform our classes in philosophy (Roben Torosyan) and art history (Marice Rose) Although we were working on the same kinds of issues (for example, developing learning goals and creating learning activities), as we implemented integrated course design, we are reporting our experiences in separate sections of this chapter.

We are indebted to Larry Miners and Kathy Nantz of Fairfield University for introducing us to Dee Fink's work, bringing Dee to campus through the Center for Academic Excellence and the Core Integration Initiative, and giving us collegial support over the years.

New Directions for Teaching and Learning, no. 119, Fall 2009 © Wiley Periodicals, Inc.
Published online in Wiley InterScience (www.interscience.wiley.com) • DOI: 10.1002/tl.365

61

Why We Changed

Both of us faced students' preconceived notions about our disciplines. And we had fallen into the rut of traditional methods of teaching in the arts and humanities, such as requiring memorization of facts and images distant to students, which do little to dispel these notions (see Figure 7.1).

Philosophy

When I say I teach philosophy, many respond, "Whoa, deep. What do you do with that anyway?" In my first philosophy course, my undergraduates reacted similarly, perceiving the requirement as simply one dead philosopher after another. After I saw Fink's (2003) six kinds of learning objectives, I wanted my students to achieve all of them, from grasping basic approaches like foundationalism and constructivism to questioning their own takes on truth, power, and ethics.

At the same time, there was pressure from the discipline to focus on rigorous primary sources and specific philosophical assumptions. Learners were not supposed to focus on personal relevance so much that they neglected to call on the thinking of philosophers explicitly. Furthermore, common cultural literacy (Hirsch, 1987) in modern and contemporary philosophy has focused on mostly Western, male philosophers. Yet as I learned about teaching for diversity and social justice (Fairfield University, 2008), I wanted to change the content to include more feminist and black authors and nontraditional perspectives.

Art History

When I tell new acquaintances that I teach art history, most respond with a variation of the following: "I took art history in college. We sat in the dark while the professor showed hundreds of slides and we frantically took notes. Flying buttresses! I wish I remembered more of it now!" The first time I taught History of Medieval Art, I similarly prepared slide lists and lectured on slide after slide. Students memorized slides for tests and researched a medieval artwork for a paper, assessments that were as tedious for me to grade as for the students to prepare and complete. I doubt that today they retain much from the course.

I wanted the course to become part of each student's intellectual and knowledge base rather than just fulfill art history's reputation as a never-ending series of slides in a dark room. I wanted students to understand how to take their art history learning and apply it to the outside world, even if they never visited the cathedrals of Europe.

What We Changed, Part I: New Learning Goals

To integrate all three components of ICD, as Fink recommends, we had to rework goals, activities, and assessments (see Figure 7.2).

Figure 7.1 The Rut: One-Way Input of Text, Visual Content, and Pet Activities

This process had to begin with the task of creating new learning goals. After reviewing what we had been doing and the results of teaching that way, we both decided that our common general learning goal was to integrate big questions with real-world applications. And that led to more specific goals for each of our courses.

Creating New Learning Goals in Philosophy

Based on Fink's taxonomy, I reformulated my learning goals as the following:

Foundational Knowledge

- Learn fundamental questions, principles, generalizations, and theories, including the use of scientific reason, the enlightenment revolution, and postmodernism.

Figure 7.2 Integrating Goals, Activities, and Assessments

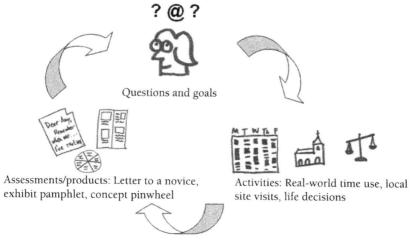

? @ ?

Questions and goals

Assessments/products: Letter to a novice, exhibit pamphlet, concept pinwheel

Activities: Real-world time use, local site visits, life decisions

- Understand twelve big philosophical questions about (1) the ethics of right and wrong, (2) our epistemologies of truth and knowledge, and (3) the metaphysics of reality and being.

Application
- Learn to analyze and critically evaluate ideas, arguments, and points of view; question assumptions (yours and others).
- Develop communication skills such as writing clearly and briefly.

Integration
- Integrate philosophical frameworks that underlie subjects and cross areas of life.

Human Dimension
- Develop a clear understanding of, and commitment to, your own philosophy and values.
- Develop confidence in your strengths and ability to reason on your own.
- Increase your sense of responsibility for serving others.

Caring
- Pursue interest in your own big philosophical questions.
- Write for thinking and for fun.
- Increase your sense of responsibility for making the world more fair.

Learning How to Learn
- Learn from mistakes, take action, and change behavior to reach goals.

Creating New Learning Goals in Art History

After attending Fink's workshop, my entire approach to the class changed—and it continues to change. My first realization was that my teaching was too content centered. The goals as written on the syllabus (for example, "You will be able to discuss medieval monuments using art historical tools and approaches") were vague and did not fully convey what I wished students to take from the class, and they did not have a clear relationship to the course's activities and assessments.

I decided to apply Fink's ICD objective of thinking about the impact of the course on the student—during the course and in the future. Following Fink's taxonomy, I created the following learning goals for my course:

Foundational Knowledge
- Students will remember the chronology of medieval art, major monuments in terms of significance and context, and art historical vocabulary.

Application
- Students will be able to take their art history learning and apply it to the outside world. For example, even if they never visit the cathedrals of Europe, students should be able to identify the relationship of architecture to religious rituals. When visiting a museum and encountering a medieval artwork that we did not study in class, students should be able to interpret its function, symbolic meaning, and significance.

NEW DIRECTIONS FOR TEACHING AND LEARNING • DOI: 10.1002/tl

Integration
- Students will relate medieval art, history, and society.

Human Dimension
- Students will become more aware of how people from various cultures, places, and times create different kinds of aesthetic environments.

Caring
- Students will be more interested in attending museums; be interested in how different people create and decorate their built environments; be excited to travel; be curious about visiting different religions' sacred structures and observing the relationship of religion to art.

Learning How to Learn
- Students will have a clear sense of what they would like to learn next about art and art history.
- They will learn about their own learning styles and how different types of activities relate.

What We Changed, Part II: Using Real-World Activities and Assessments

New learning goals inevitably require new learning and assessment activities. Our new goals made us realize we needed to get out of the classroom, figuratively and literally. They also forced us to reconsider the function of all our learning and assessment activities. We needed to reconsider how we wanted students to use their textbooks. Organizing learning activities around questions, for example, would allow students to apply knowledge rather than just regurgitate it. Reducing reading assignments let us focus on how well students used course material in the world outside class. And having students work together to complete many assessments, often creatively, taught them teamwork and collaboration skills.

Learning Activities in Philosophy

When I initially began the process of redesigning my course, I unfortunately fell into the rut of using favorite activities without clearly connecting them to learning objectives. Even when I listed learning objectives, I did not design backward from there to ask how I would know when students accomplished those results.

To correct that problem, I began with creating learning activities for foundational knowledge. I organized the activities less around completing readings and more around asking big questions, such as these:

- How do we know right from wrong?
- Is certainty possible?
- What is really real?

Because students rarely completed readings, and even when they did, they misunderstood the most basic concepts, I reduced the reading assignments by approximately 50 percent. This focus on quality over quantity to fulfill the foundational knowledge goals sometimes meant assigning only seven pages a week when we were tackling difficult material.

To encourage close reading of texts, I had groups take different reading sections, capture main points with examples, and generate a question for discussion. Finally, before summing up key points each session, I asked groups to come up with a metaphor, haiku, visual scribble, or skit to capture what they saw as vital insights.

For one application activity, students were to apply course concepts to improve thinking, problem-solving, and decision-making skills. In order to elicit real-world improvement of such personal activities, learners kept a twenty-four-hour time line of how free or determined they felt and behaved in fifteen-minute increments, inspired by how Fink had his students note the geography behind everything they see and touch in a day.

A second application activity asked students to analyze and critically evaluate ideas, arguments, and points of view. I asked them to write a letter to a philosophical novice. The task had students working to teach a key question to someone outside the class. In the letter, they were to pose a key question, analyze it using an example from personal life, and represent an opposing viewpoint fairly.

I used small groups to support the application goal of improving students' writing skills. Using peer feedback, they practiced stages of brainstorming, rethinking their whole approach, moving big pieces around, and fine proofreading.

Learning Activities in Art History

One of the difficulties of teaching a medieval art class is that students do not have a previous interest in the course content, which ranges from early Christian catacombs to Gothic cathedrals. Nor do they find it relevant to their twenty-first-century lives. In order to make the class more relevant to the students, I revised learning goals. Class format, activities, and assessments therefore needed to focus on big questions that are not restricted to the medieval period—for example:

- What is the relationship of belief, ritual, and community to religious art and architecture?
- What is the impact of pilgrimage on art and architecture?

I lectured less in the classroom, trusting that students were receiving foundational information from reading assignments. It was reassuring to know that content learning was not lost. For example, knowledge of canonical medieval monuments is one of the foundational course goals.

NEW DIRECTIONS FOR TEACHING AND LEARNING • DOI: 10.1002/tl

However, I reduced the number of monuments for which students were responsible. I also reduced the percentage of the final grade that slide-based quizzes were worth. The focus now is more on students' writing up activity results and reflections.

To help students relate better to the textbook material, we went outside the classroom to visit a Greek Orthodox church, where we studied icons and domes. With this activity, the class was acquiring and reinforcing their foundational knowledge.

One excellent example of student-centered learning was an assignment that required students to develop a cohesive medieval art exhibition. Working in teams, students chose a theme like "the Virgin Mary." They selected works of art from varied times and places, drew a gallery plan explaining placement and relationships of the artworks, composed a letter to the university president explaining why the exhibit deserved support, and brainstormed educational outreach events for fellow students and community members. These assessments were especially authentic, as they were similar to a museum professional's activities.

Another activity asked students to apply learning about the Middle Ages to the present. Students chose a modern pilgrimage site and researched and wrote papers comparing the modern site to a medieval one. Another assignment had students using art historical vocabulary to compare a religious building in their home town to a religious building in medieval times.

These activities were meaningful and relevant because they brought medieval art into the students' era. The activities were also more personal because students took greater ownership when they were responsible for choosing artworks to include or exclude.

What Happened

With the redesign of our courses, an important outcome was that students seemed to find our new goals relevant to contemporary living. They became inventive in undertaking generative activities as they made the big questions meaningful and applied course content to real-world observations. In fact, a new energy became palpable in our classrooms.

Results of the Changes in Philosophy

During my first year of changing this course, students' goals surprisingly matched most of mine. Since many were graduating seniors, most wanted, for example, to figure out the human dimension of "what to do with my life" after graduation. Student letters to a novice also explained foundational concepts, although not with great critical reflection.

When students generated haiku and visual representations, the outcomes surprised me as well as guest presenters. Students excelled as they translated complex concepts like meta-reflexivity and deconstruction into devices like pinwheels and cartoon cards recursively pointing to one another, showing integration of concepts.

A human dimension goal had students respond to readings personally by posting in online discussions an example of how they were prompted to question their own philosophical values and assumptions. When students thus found relevant application of otherwise turgid material, they became energized and engaged. They addressed specific incidents, like times they were generous or altruistic, by asking when enjoying an act interferes with staying morally committed on principle. Many students saw more paradoxes, like how they chose to study or work out, and yet were also determined by heredity and environment—under pressure from parents and peers.

Results of the Changes in Art History

In the first semester using ICD, there was significantly more energy in the classroom due to the decrease in lecturing and increase in group work and discussion. Students clearly spent more time on their projects than on the previous research paper assignment. I was particularly impressed with the results of the projects relating medieval architecture and pilgrimage to the present day. Each fulfilled the application, integration, human dimension, and foundational knowledge goals.

Furthermore, although creativity had not been a learning objective, I saw wonderful examples of it as students produced educational pamphlets for their exhibitions and wrote some papers from a medieval pilgrim's viewpoint. Another unforeseen bonus was that I looked forward to reading their work and learned a great deal myself. For example, I had not known that contemporary Girl Scout troop visits to founder Juliette Low's house in Savannah include most of the features of a medieval religious pilgrimage.

These projects required more collaboration and discussion than previously assigned research papers. Instead of passively absorbing information from a podium, students were learning from one another. By sharing their work, they learned different ways to synthesize the material, which helped in their learning how to learn.

Our Learning

Despite the positive results from our initial changes, we both discovered that we needed to refine our course designs not once but continually, to improve both student engagement and our own. We continue to try to strike the right balance between foundational knowledge and our other significant learning goals. We still find that transparency about our course goals is essential, both for the students to learn and for us to teach effectively.

Philosophy

By my third year, my grading criteria became more specific, as I posted sample student work, pointing out where writing reached my learning objectives well or inadequately. The students' letters to a novice then improved: many students hooked the addressee's interest, explained a philosophical concept or dilemma clearly, or gave a concrete example from actual experience. Most important, students questioned their own points of view more—sometimes even dearly held beliefs.

I have learned that I should better prepare students for the hardest parts of thinking and writing; for example, how to take a perspective that is not easily torn down. I also need to have individual classes develop a rubric with sample phrases that demonstrate each criterion.

One problem that concerned me was that most students could not remember anything specific to any philosopher. I need to link the ideas of actual philosophers to students' thinking. If not, "What would Descartes say?" I could at least ask, "What do *you* say, and how does Descartes *help?*"

To better convey the urgent need for justice, sustainability, and diversity awareness, I need to push students beyond simply noticing and questioning things, to asking, "How will I make a difference, here and now?" (Fairfield University, 2008).

To reach this and other goals, I keep relearning the need to decide two or three things students should learn each session and put them on the board with an agenda.

Overall, then, the more freedom students have, combined with a clear sense of what is expected of them, the more they may thrive and I may renew my methods of working with them.

Art History

The transition was not flawless. I was not prepared for moderating class discussions and grading more creative projects. I was not transparent enough in my motivations in introducing student-centered learning in class. Some students wrote in the course evaluations that the in-class group projects "felt like busywork"; one student wrote, "I like the format of every other art history class I have taken much more than this one."

By the second time I taught the course, I trusted students to take the lead in discussion, even asking them to moderate in-class debates. I became better at providing rubrics and examples with assignments, and at addressing their need to know what I was looking for in nontraditional projects.

I brought back more lecture, but was careful not to repeat but to clarify and expand what was in the textbook, and I included more textbook-based questions on quizzes to ensure that students were responsible for completing readings to obtain foundational knowledge. The balance seems to be successful; one student wrote, "I like the style of teaching—the combination of lecture, readings, and projects made the class interesting. I feel like I learned a lot from this course."

I have to keep reminding myself to explain the course goals and how class activities and assessments relate to them, for both my own focus and my students' own learning. I need to balance teaching students how to think like an art historian by giving them tools to consider the art that is part of their everyday lives. I want them to not only be able to identify a Gothic flying buttress but to see how it relates to their spatial experience inside Chartres Cathedral as they travel abroad after graduation and to understand why their home town churches do not have flying buttresses.

Despite my continuous revising of the course, the one constant is that now no student who takes a class with me can truthfully say that art history is about spitting out what they memorized in a dark room.

Conclusion

We shifted core courses in modern philosophy and medieval art history from focusing on readings and papers to examining big questions about personal beliefs and values and integrating learning with lives in motion. Innovations included reading less but more deeply, using personalized questions to apply learning to life, and designing exhibitions and other visual products organized around student-chosen themes.

Evidence showed that learners gained interest, internalized knowledge creatively, and found relevance in subjects that can often alienate the uninitiated. Furthermore, we realized ways to winnow objectives and specify guidelines and models for student work, while continuing to renew our own engagement with the teaching.

References

Fairfield University. "Diversity and Social Justice, Living and Learning Community Housing." 2008. Retrieved Sept. 10, 2008, from http://www.fairfield.edu/res_living learning.html.

Fink, L. D. *Creating Significant Learning Experiences: An Integrated Approach to Designing College Courses.* San Francisco: Jossey-Bass, 2003.

Hirsch, E. D., Jr. *Cultural Literacy: What Every American Should Know.* Boston: Houghton Mifflin, 1987.

MARICE ROSE *is assistant professor of art history at Fairfield University in Connecticut. E-mail: mrose@fairfield.edu.*

ROBEN TOROSYAN *is associate director of the Center for Academic Excellence and assistant professor of curriculum and instruction at Fairfield University in Connecticut. E-mail: rtorosyan@fairfield.edu.*

The students in a virology course helped set the learning goals, and the design and content of the exams, and they developed rubrics for individual and group projects. The result was that they learned how to direct their own learning.

Integrated Design of a Virology Course Develops Lifelong Learners

Joseph C. Mester

After my first year of full-time teaching in the Department of Biological Sciences at Northern Kentucky University (NKU), I was fortunate to learn about integrated course design at a workshop on our campus led by Dee Fink. I had taught for four years as a graduate student (and for three additional years as an adjunct professor) and had never taken a course in teaching theory or course design. As a result, my lecture courses emphasized coverage of scientific facts and concepts (foundation knowledge). While doing this in a manner that I hoped was engaging and sometimes entertaining, I felt there was room for improvement as far as student outcomes, especially in long-term knowledge retention.

In addition to wanting to make sure that I was being an effective instructor, I knew that I had a special challenge on the immediate horizon. In the upcoming semester, I was scheduled to teach an upper-level course on virology (the study of viruses). The class would meet three times a week in an intimate setting (twelve students) and would not have laboratory exercises. All of the scientific courses that I had previously taught were more introductory and included directly linked laboratory exercises. Students usually stated that the laboratory exercises were the most enjoyable aspect

Thanks to Sabine Zacate for sharing her experience as the instructor of a virology course, Doug Robertson for his encouragement and support, and Dee and Arletta Fink for their guidance and critical reading of the manuscript for this chapter.

of the course and frequently stated that they did not fully understand the course material until they had a chance to see it in action in the lab.

Integrated Course Design

My mission was both exciting and challenging: design a new upper-level course from the ground up and include meaningful learning experiences that compensated for the lack of an associated laboratory section. Having learned about integrated course design, I wanted to build in additional learning goals, including those involving the human dimension and lifelong learning, and determine their contribution to student outcomes.

As part of the integrated design, all of my course goals targeted long-term outcomes, which was refreshingly relevant. Early in my teaching career, I already felt that too much emphasis was being placed on the short-term cramming of information. It should not have been surprising, then, that students in general cared only about what was on the next exam, while at the same time, my colleagues and I complained about students who showed little knowledge retention from semester to semester. Remarkably, through the implementation of integrated course design, this situation would improve dramatically.

Designing the Course

The course design took place during a two-day workshop led by Dee Fink with other faculty at NKU. The workshop involved a combination of brief presentations, individual planning (guided by worksheets), brainstorming sessions in small and large groups, and reflection activities. Interaction with, and feedback from, other faculty and Dee were invaluable for sparking new ideas and later molding them into final form.

In planning the course, I targeted six learning goal areas: foundation knowledge, application, integration and synthesis, the human dimension, caring, and learning how to learn (Fink, 2003). The activities within these areas, while mainly assessed during the course, targeted long-range outcomes of a year or more after course completion. Essentially the activities were designed to set the stage for and encourage continued study after the course was completed. A summary of the course goals, assessments, and activities is shown in Table 8.1.

Setting Course Goals

Students were encouraged from the beginning to become self-directed learners. For example, they were involved in setting the course objectives by submitting their ideas in the first week of class. The final objectives were discussed and vetted by all at the beginning of the second week of class. Student feedback was also sought for exam design and content, and the class developed metrics for grading the individual and group projects before they were submitted.

Table 8.1 Three-Column Table for the Virology Course

Learning Goals	Assessment	Activities
Foundation knowledge: Acquire in-depth knowledge of key concepts of virology. Familiarity with and use of major medical and virology research journals.	Exams Written assignments Individual presentations Group project	Independent reading and literature research Multimedia in-class presentations Attendance at scientific seminars Participation in scientific poster sessions Student collaboration
Application: Apply course knowledge creatively and critically to solve current medical problems. Demonstrate teamwork in preparing a complex project.	Exams Written assignments Individual presentations Group project	Preparation of two reports on current topics Student-derived lecture materials Preparation and presentation of group project
Integration and synthesis: Understand the various levels of virus-host interactions. Assess the contributions of virology to advances in science and medicine.	Exams Written assignments Individual presentations Group project	Independent reading and literature research Student-derived lecture materials In-class discussion Preparation and presentation of group project
Human dimension: Gain historical and human perspective of key advances in virology. Value the group learning environment.	Exams Written assignments Individual presentations Group project	Independent reading and literature research Student-derived lecture materials In-class discussion Student collaboration
Caring: Understand the impact of viral disease on individuals and populations. Value the group learning environment.	Exams Written assignments Individual presentations Group project	Group project focus on disease epidemiology at the local, national, and worldwide levels In-class discussion
Lifelong learning: Gain long-term interest in virology. Gain an appreciation of the benefits of virology research to society. Learn to think as a scientist.	Current topics reports Group project Follow-up with individual class members after completion of course	Independent reading and literature research Preparation of two reports on current topics and group project Discussion of current topics inside and outside class

NEW DIRECTIONS FOR TEACHING AND LEARNING • DOI: 10.1002/tl

Learning Assignments and Assessments

The activities and assessments were designed as rich learning experiences that involved multiple learning goals. For example, the activity of independent reading and literature research, which was emphasized early and throughout the course, strengthened the understanding of foundation knowledge, fostered integration and synthesis, and developed independent learning tools for the pursuit of lifelong learning. As a guide for this activity, I frequently scanned the major medical and virology journals, along with the popular press, for current articles of interest and posted them on the network for the students to read. These articles served as supporting material for the course text or other activities. I also frequently discussed and recommended other relevant sources of information that were available on the Web. As the course progressed, the students cited current content that they found and discussed its implications for the class.

Assignments and Assessments for Multiple Learning Goals

For an assessment that covered multiple learning goals, the students were assigned focused topics to research individually at approximately one-month intervals. They then were asked to build a slide-based lecture presentation on that topic. The focused topics were part of an overall lecture theme, such as herpes virus–based vaccines and gene therapy vectors. The students were given approximately two weeks to assemble their brief lecture presentations, which were usually composed of two to four slides per student. Before the lecture, the students e-mailed their slides to me, and I reviewed and assembled them into a single slide show. In this way, several lectures were mainly student derived (with some instructor editing), with all students contributing to the content. The students briefly presented their slides to the class and then led discussions of the material at the end of their presentations.

This activity was graded as an assignment/homework activity. The course had six assignments that together counted toward 15 percent of the final grade. Notably, this assessment encompassed a majority of the course's learning goal areas (shown in Table 8.1). Without exception, the students embraced and excelled at this type of assignment, going into greater depth and detail than I originally anticipated.

Additional Assignments

The students were given assignments to attend talks on campus by visiting medical scientists who presented their research in detailed seminars. To receive assignment credit, the students wrote a one-page summary of the presenter's work. Quite often the students related the work to their personal interests or situations, such as knowing someone who had that disorder and how the scientific developments highlighted in the talk may someday lead to a cure for it.

NEW DIRECTIONS FOR TEACHING AND LEARNING • DOI: 10.1002/tl

From the perspective of foundation knowledge, application, and integration, these talks were valuable for their presentations of the scientific method and current research techniques. From the human and caring dimension, the talks often embraced ethical and other current issues in science, such as the current controversy over stem cell research. These issues clearly stood out and were actively embraced in the student summaries.

Our department also hosts several undergraduate research poster sessions during the semester. The students were given assignments to attend the poster sessions, discuss the experimental approaches with the authors, and then apply those techniques to novel student-proposed virology research projects. This resulted in several surprisingly excellent approaches authored by the students for solving current problems in experimental virology. These outside-of-class activities and assessments opened doors to many new avenues of learning.

Periodic review and synthesis sessions were done in class with whiteboard summaries of class discussions. One such session focused on the desired (good) and undesired (bad) aspects of antiviral vaccines and drugs, with the question being, "How would you design an effective antiviral drug or vaccine?" These types of discussions emphasized the importance of a group approach to problem solving and the value of new ideas and approaches in problem solving.

Bringing the Laboratory into the Classroom

My approach to cover the lack of an associated laboratory was three-pronged: using in-class and out-of-class activities involving observation, interaction, and the write-up or oral presentation of results (or both). My primary goal was to bring the laboratory into the lecture and promote participation in activities outside class that emphasized experimental techniques.

Discussions within the class focused on the experimental push-and-pull, the early controversies, and the scientific debate behind major theories. These kinds of discussions helped to encourage the view of current science as a dynamic and actively evolving endeavor rather than a fact-laden and slowly changing enterprise. Detailed experimental techniques were described, with comments on their ease of use, along with how to interpret results accurately and how to potentially improve the procedures. Actual materials and photographs of laboratory equipment were used for demonstrations.

Enhancing Integration

Integration of course content was taking place as students were learning that viruses are wonderful tools for understanding how genes and cells work. In addition, my more than twenty years of experience at the bench in academic, clinical, and pharmaceutical research allowed me to draw on my personal experience when describing real-world applications.

The class discussed how the various experimental techniques are applied, and the personal and human perspective of what is fun and easy to do or more painstakingly laborious. Because of the varied scientific depth of background of the students, discussions toggled from superficial to deeper layers. Students truly enjoyed the less formal and candid assessments of various laboratory techniques, demonstrating how the human perspective can make otherwise dry material more personal and approachable.

Much of the course work was done parallel to and culminated with the completion of a large group project. The group projects focused on one of three viruses that are currently major threats to human health: pandemic influenza virus, human immunodeficiency virus, and hepatitis C virus. The group or team was responsible for all activities involved in the preparation and submission of a written and an oral report detailing the current state of the human health burden of the virus and potential solutions for its treatment and prevention. The goal of the project was to provide detailed scientific descriptions of (1) the virus; (2) the impact and epidemiology of the pandemic at the worldwide, national, and local levels; (3) current and future methods for prevention; and (4) current and future methods for treatment.

The team projects were initiated early and developed throughout the course. The grade on each project was 15 percent of the final grade and was assessed as described in *Team-Based Learning* (Michaelsen and Fink, 2004).

How the Course Design Worked

Overall, the students actively participated in the course activities and classroom discussions and demonstrated enhanced performance in assessments by going beyond expectations in the depth of their work. The experimental slant of discussions encouraged students to take risks and use their ongoing studies or job experiences to suggest new approaches for problem solving. Including the human dimension made the course more personal and the students more committed to their assignments and assessments. Most impressive, they continue to stop by my office to discuss the latest in virology, their new classes, and their careers. The evidence of enhanced student learning due to integrated course design is summarized in Table 8.2.

Individual Writing Assignments

In general, the use of small writing assignments based on out-of-class activities yielded the most promising results. All of the students embraced the current topic reports with great enthusiasm, demonstrating that they were extremely curious and capable of individually researching and reporting on a variety of topics. Quite often they went far beyond the course content and explored exotic and emerging viruses, potential bioterror agents, prions, and the challenges of successfully vaccinating an aging population against viral diseases.

NEW DIRECTIONS FOR TEACHING AND LEARNING • DOI: 10.1002/tl

Table 8.2 Impact of ICD on Student Learning

Learning Goals	Evidence of Student Learning	Relationship to Changes in Overall Course Design
Foundation knowledge	Enhanced performance on exams and assignments. Greater depth in exam responses and in individual and group projects.	Students were empowered to learn without bounds, follow their interests, and excel in their studies.
Application	Highly creative application of established procedures during problem-solving assignments.	Students were challenged to think creatively and find novel solutions to current problems.
Integration and synthesis	Class discussions showed that students were connecting the course knowledge to other courses, their undergraduate research projects, their jobs, and their personal lives.	Rich learning experiences and a holistic approach made it easier for the students to see the big picture while learning the intimate details of the course work.
Human dimension and caring	Student-led scientific discussions always included the human perspective (epidemiological and personal impact, historical relevance).	Emphasized for the first time by this instructor. Paid off handsomely in terms of greater student engagement.
Lifelong learning	Discussions in and out of class gave evidence of reflective thinking. Students continue to stop by my office to drop off news and articles of interest and discuss related topics almost one year after the course ended.	The end result of effective course design.

Assigned attendance at undergraduate research poster sessions, with the purpose of finding new approaches for investigative virology, yielded great dividends. This is a technique practiced by savvy scientists who are always on the lookout for new approaches and ideas. This encouraged and resulted in truly novel student-authored approaches for solving current problems in experimental virology.

Group Research Project

The group project saw great effort by most individuals, but it never quite jelled. Each team was composed of four students, and in each case individual members picked one aspect of the four-part problem to address, even though it was stressed that it was not necessary to approach the project this way. Each student wrote his or her report and composed a slide-based presentation mostly independently of the others. One student became the organizer who compiled everything for submission.

The projects suffered somewhat by a lack of continuity and integration. Another problem became evident when one person in each of two of the teams did not contribute anything to the project. It appeared that in each case, the student assured team members that he or she was working on his or her component of the project and was on schedule for timely completion, but when it came time to deliver the work to the team, the student had not completed his or her part. The organizer for the group then had to perform a speedy repair for the missing item, and the project reports and presentations suffered accordingly. The remaining team, where everyone contributed to the final project, delivered an impressive, thorough, and emotionally moving report and presentation. The epidemiology section was especially well done, which made the impact of viral diseases feel very personal.

Course Examinations

The students' level of commitment to the course material was clearly evident during the course examinations. Compared to previous courses, the students spent much more time completing their exams. Three in-class exams were given, with each exam counting 20 percent of the final grade. For the second and third exams, the number of questions was reduced relative to the previous exam to minimize the amount of time required, yet the students still spent about two hours each time completing them. Impressively, most students used independently garnered information or examples from outside class in their answers.

Improved Grades

Exam averages for the course were in the mid- to low 80s (out of 100 points). Excellent performance was evident in the individual reports and assignments, with averages in the mid- to low 90s. Individual scores from the group project averaged in mid- to high 80s. The overall course average grade was in the high 80s.

In related microbiology courses taught at NKU, the overall course average grade is usually in the low 80s. The previous virology class, which focused mainly on foundation knowledge, had three written exams and one major oral or written presentation, and the overall course average was in the low to mid-80s.

While overall grade performance was enhanced by one-half of a letter grade, the most important outcome was strong evidence of independent learning and student submersion in the material.

What I Learned

Integrated course design and implementation of rich student learning experiences dramatically enhanced the scholarship of both students and the instructor. It allowed full immersion of the students in the course material and made the course a living entity that continued to breathe past the final exam. Particularly, learning goals linked to caring and the human dimension, which are often overlooked in the scientific curriculum, were powerful motivators and integrators.

The encouragement of creative, independent, and applied thinking was greatly rewarded. Overall, shorter student projects were more successful than larger ones. The larger group project yielded less consistent engagement by the students as a whole. The design of the group project was too broad in scope, too easily divided into individual components, and not fully focused on group-based problem solving.

A better design for the group project would place less emphasis on covering background information and more emphasis on creating novel solutions for preventing and treating viral disease. Having all of the groups focus on one topic, such as pandemic influenza, would enhance individual and group effort (Michaelsen and Knight, 2004). I would give the groups more time during class to brainstorm their ideas; then I would give them time to write up summaries of their solutions on flip-chart paper. Following this, the groups would simultaneously post their written summaries on the wall. These procedures should stimulate greater intergroup discussion regarding their different solutions to the same problem. A smaller summary write-up from each student would encourage them to reflect on what they learned from the project.

This was my first attempt at integrated course design, and I found it to be greatly rewarding for both the students and myself. Even without associated laboratory exercises, student engagement and learning were high. I plan on applying integrated course design to my other science courses, to enhance learning and develop students who are lifelong learners.

References

Fink, L. D. *Creating Significant Learning Experiences: An Integrated Approach to Designing College Courses.* San Francisco: Jossey-Bass, 2003.

Michaelsen, L. K., and Fink, L. D. "Calculating Peer Evaluation Scores." In L. K. Michaelsen, A. B. Knight, and L. D. Fink (eds.), *Team-Based Learning: A Transformative Use of Small Groups in College Teaching.* Sterling, Va.: Stylus, 2004.

Michaelsen, L. K., and Knight, A. B. "Creating Effective Assignments: A Key Component of Team-Based Learning." In L. K. Michaelsen, A. B. Knight, and L. D. Fink (eds.), *Team-Based Learning: A Transformative Use of Small Groups in College Teaching.* Sterling, Va.: Stylus, 2004.

JOSEPH C. MESTER is an assistant professor in the Department of Biological Sciences at Northern Kentucky University. E-mail: mesterj1@nku.edu.

NEW DIRECTIONS FOR TEACHING AND LEARNING • DOI: 10.1002/tl

Instead of tinkering with minor changes, the author used integrated course design as a blueprint for a major overhaul of her course.

An "Extreme Makeover" of a Course in Special Education

Joan M. Nicoll-Senft

Just as the popular television show *Extreme Makeover: Home Edition* (Endemol, 2003) targets the demolition and reconstruction of a home so that it better meets the needs of its owners, Fink's approach to integrated course design (ICD; 2003) provides higher education faculty with the tools to deconstruct and do a major remodel of their college courses. Teaching responsibilities, coupled with a seemingly endless array of other university duties, often prevent faculty from such remodeling endeavors. Instead, we make a change here or there, overwhelmed by the task of thinking beyond these piecemeal changes. Fink's ICD model, however, provides a blueprint for faculty who are ready and willing to roll up their sleeves and remodel.

The Need for Change

As a junior faculty member, I found myself in need of such remodeling. I was a bit overwhelmed by the task of teaching a course that would prepare future special education teachers to plan instruction for students with disabilities. How could I effectively prepare my students to plan instruction for students with a wide range of disabilities, from elementary through high school, in one three-credit class? After two or three semesters, the answer was clear: I could not. My approach was a heavy emphasis on lecturing, with few opportunities for active learning, and still I could not squeeze in all of the necessary content.

NEW DIRECTIONS FOR TEACHING AND LEARNING, no. 119, Fall 2009 © Wiley Periodicals, Inc.
Published online in Wiley InterScience (www.interscience.wiley.com) • DOI: 10.1002/tl.367

At the same time I was struggling with teaching this course, I became involved in a scholarship of teaching and learning (SoTL) project to implement and evaluate Fink's ICD model that evolved out of our university's book club. As a result, I learned it is possible to teach students how to apply and integrate new knowledge and be self-directed learners by responding to a series of challenging situations that special education teachers face.

What I Did: My Course Demolition and Remodeling Process

I used Fink's model of ICD to remodel a three-credit graduate-level course that leads to special education certification. This course focuses on developing individualized education plans (IEP) and subsequent lesson plans to meet the needs of students with disabilities. The class met weekly for two hours and forty minutes with a typical enrollment of approximately twenty students.

Situational Factors

When remodeling, first it is necessary to identify the unique challenges of the situation. Consequently, Fink's method of ICD begins by identifying the important situational factors of a course. As in many other college courses, the biggest challenge with this one was the breadth of subject matter covered. In Connecticut, as in many other states, students receiving an initial endorsement in special education receive a noncategorical K–12 special education teaching certificate. Therefore, course content spans planning instruction from elementary school through high school, covering a wide range of disabilities—from students with mild learning disabilities, to students who are intellectually disabled, behaviorally challenged, or are gifted and talented.

Coupled with this breadth of content is the varying degree to which students differ in their background knowledge and teaching experiences. In a typical semester, approximately one-third of the students enrolled in this course are experienced general education teachers. Another third of the class is made up of students who recently received a general education teaching certificate and are pursuing a master's degree prior to beginning their teaching career. The remaining students are postbaccalaureate students with little or no training or experience in teaching. Furthermore, since this is a course that leads to special education teacher certification, state and national standards dictate specific competencies that students must master regardless of prior training or teaching experience. Finally, course content is tied to high-stakes testing necessary to obtain a state-issued teaching certificate.

New Learning Goals

The foundation of Fink's model is the development of course goals based on a taxonomy that goes beyond rote knowledge and application of skills toward the development of self-directed learners. Fink describes six categories of significant learning: foundational knowledge, application, integration, the human dimension, caring, and learning how to learn.

Using Fink's taxonomy, I reduced the overall number of course goals while extending foundational knowledge and application of that knowledge to areas that I never considered before, such as caring and learning how to learn. Table 9.1 contains a list of my new course goals.

Assignments That Assess

Perhaps even more significant than Fink's taxonomy of learning is his triangulation of learning goals, assessments, and teaching and learning activities (Fink, 2003). Once I had developed course goals, I designed assignments that would directly assess each of these goals. Assignments ranged from informal student learning logs to complex group projects. Inspired by Fink's planning process, I incorporated these goals and their related assessments in the course syllabus. (Table 9.1 contains a complete list of course goals and assessments.) Students thus had a clear understanding of course goals

Table 9.1 Course Goals and Assessments Using Fink's Taxonomy

Taxa	Course Goals	Assessment
Foundational knowledge	Identify the components and stages of the IEP process, including demonstrating the ability to write standards-based, measurable IEP goals, and objectives.	Develop or rewrite an appropriate IEP including goals and objectives.
Application	Demonstrate the ability to develop appropriate accommodations or modifications, or both, in order to ensure appropriate access to the general education curriculum.	Student learning profile Lesson plan
Integration	Develop a universally designed teaching unit consisting of five lesson plans that are aligned with national, state, and local curricula standards.	Teaching unit
Human dimension	Demonstrate an understanding of their own strengths and challenges and learning style as well as those of the students they teach.	Problem-based learning (PBL) reflection papers and PBL feedback forms
Caring	Demonstrate an interest in learning about current educational trends and issues and their impact on students with exceptionalities.	Student logs
Learning how to learn	Reflect on one's teaching to improve instruction and guide professional growth.	Reflection paper

and how their mastery of these goals would be measured. This systematic planning process ensures that course assessments are balanced and an integral part of the overall course design, not just the standard midterm and final.

Teaching and Learning Activities

After this planning came the selection of appropriate teaching and learning activities. How could I possibly teach this course so that students would achieve the goals I so carefully developed? In his ICD model, Fink recommends the selection or creation of an overall teaching strategy. After considerable reflection and research, I selected problem-based learning (PBL) as a teaching strategy for the course.

Problem-Based Learning: A Teaching Strategy

Developed over thirty years ago to teach first- and second-year medical students (Albanese and Mitchell, 1993), PBL has been extended to undergraduate and graduate education and even elementary and secondary school settings. Barrows (1996) defines the central characteristics of PBL as (1) student-centered learning, (2) learning in small groups, (3) the use of tutors to serve as facilitators or guides, (4) authentic problems presented prior to preparation or study, (5) use of problem-solving skills, and (6) new information acquired through self-directed learning.

Using my course goals as my blueprint, I developed three problems that served as the framework for this course. Problems were developed based on actual situations I have faced as a teacher, administrator, or educational consultant. The design of engaging, complex problems is central to PBL, as these problems form the basis of ongoing student work. Problems were introduced to students at the beginning of each unit of study throughout the semester. Each problem contained a brief scenario that introduced the problem, a description of the group's assignment related to the problem, and suggestions for sharing student work related to the problem at the end of each unit of study.

Group Assignment

At the beginning of the semester, students were assigned to permanent heterogeneous groups. Group assignment was based on each student's prior teaching experience and the grade level he or she currently taught or was interested in teaching. Students were assigned to one of four groups: early childhood, elementary, middle school, or high school. Each group consisted of four to six students, at least one of whom was a full-time teacher. The other group members had expressed an interest in teaching at that grade level but had little to no teaching experience.

Individual Accountability

In order to ensure individual accountability, student logs were used to document each student's individual contributions to their group. I informally reviewed the logs at the beginning of each class and formally graded them at the end of the semester. To make this a manageable end-of-semester grading process, students were directed to identify one log from each problem that they felt best reflected their contribution to their group. I also informed them that I would read (and grade) this student-selected log along with a randomly selected log from each problem to determine their overall grade for this assignment.

Assessment

Since this course remodeling process was part of a larger university-wide Scholarship of Teaching and Learning (SoTL) project, course-specific pre- and postassessments were developed to assess student learning in relation to Fink's taxonomy. Although the content of these assessments differed from course to course, in general they consisted of multiple-choice questions, Likert scale survey questions, and short essay questions. Pre- and post-assessments were administered in class and took approximately one hour for students to complete. The preassessment was administered during the first class session, and the postassessment was administered on the final day of class. Only students who completed both assessments were included in the data analysis. The pre- and postassessments were scored by research assistants who were unaware of the purpose of the study.

Results: "Move That Bus So We Can See the Results!"

In one point in each edition of the *Extreme Makeover* TV program, participants shout out, "Move that bus," so they can see the results of the house remodel. What were the results of my remodeled course?

Data Analysis

Students' scores on pre- and postassessments were analyzed to look for significant improvement in student learning in each of Fink's areas of significant learning. Scores from the pre- and postsemester assessments were compared using paired (by student) t-tests at $\alpha = 0.05$. Positive changes in student learning were found in each of the six areas, with the changes being statistically significant in four areas: application, integration, the human dimension, and learning to learn (see Table 9.2). These data provide support for the ICD model as a method of course design capable of creating significant learning for students in higher education.

Although changes in student performance on the pre- and postassessments in foundational knowledge were not statistically significant, the more important aspects of application and integration of foundational knowledge did result in significant changes. The problem-based nature of the course most likely contributed to the significant learning found in these areas. The lack of significance in caring may have been due to difficulties in operationalizing and therefore measuring this area. Moreover, student scores in

Table 9.2 P Values for Pretests and Posttests

Taxa	Pre-Redesigned Course	Post-Redesigned Course
Foundational knowledge	.0276	.3950
Application	.0004	.0075*
Integration	.1026	.0006*
Human dimension	.0066	.0115*
Caring	.1851	.3347
Learning to learn	.0934	.0117*

*P values with an asterisk are statistically significant at α = .05.

this taxon were near the ceiling and therefore had limited potential to increase.

Course Evaluation
In addition to assessing the remodeled course in terms of student learning, student reactions to the course were assessed by course evaluations. The course evaluation form that the Department of Special Education used consists of seventeen positively worded statements that students respond to by strongly agreeing, agreeing, disagreeing, or strongly disagreeing. In the course evaluation forms, 100 percent of the students strongly agreed or agreed with all seventeen statements on the department's evaluation form. In addition to responding to each statement, students wrote individual comments on the form. The following are examples of these comments: "very well organized," "interested in students' progress," "this class was a great learning experience," and "taking this class was a great personal experience for me."

Reflections After the Dust Has Settled

As a result of this project, I found that it is possible to have an impact on student learning on many levels, well beyond foundational knowledge, by using ICD. Using Fink's taxonomy in the development of course goals and assessments, and ultimately in my teaching, strengthened my course and resulted in a much deeper learning experience for students. The breadth of the goals developed for this course using the taxonomy opened new doors to course assessments and approaches to teaching that I had not previously considered. My students also appreciated the clarity and readability of course goals and their explicit alignment with course assessments.

Teamwork and Problem-Solving Skills
I found that students had had surprisingly limited experiences in working together in small groups. They needed to learn how to make optimal use of their time and resources both in and out of class. Knowing how to organize their work, distribute the workload evenly, and communicate with their

group members outside class were tasks that students identified in their student logs as areas they continued to work on throughout the semester. Over time, they began to improve in these areas as they worked on more complex problems and developed multifaceted assignments as a result of their individual and group work.

Self-Directed Learners

I found that initially students were lacking in their ability to be self-directed in their learning. Weekly meetings with student groups, coupled with the use of student logs, allowed me to identify and address these issues with students. As the semester continued, student groups became more efficient in their individual and group efforts as the problems presented to them grew in complexity.

Shifting Roles for Me as a Teacher

One important lesson for me was the frontloaded nature of this method of course design; it required considerable reflection and planning before the course began. Gone are the days of pondering about the content and structure of a final exam just days before the end of the semester. Identifying the scope and sequence of engaging problems was also time-consuming, but once the problems were developed, my preparation time during the semester was minimal.

My role as a teacher shifted from covering course content to that of being a facilitator of student learning. Every week I spent class time meeting with small groups of students to answer questions and assist students in their ongoing work. In this capacity, I assisted students in identifying and locating resource material pertaining to their problem and often gave students feedback on their individual and group work. As my role changed, so did the role of my students. They were no longer passive learners but instead became active problem solvers.

Conclusion

The most important test of a model such as this is whether it withstands the test of time. Three years later, I continue to use the ICD model. Actually I find it difficult not to use it, especially the backward nature of course planning. I continue to rely on Fink's taxonomy when creating course goals, and a table that aligns course goals and assessments has become a standard fixture in my course syllabi. As a teacher trainer, I find it important to walk my talk in planning and teaching, and ICD has provided me with an established framework for this process.

References

Albanese, M. A., and Mitchell, S. "Problem-Based Learning: A Review of Literature on Its Outcomes and Implementation Issues." *Academic Medicine,* 1993, *68,* 52–81.

Barrows, H. S. "Problem-Based Learning in Medicine and Beyond." In L. Wilerson and W. H. Gijselaers (eds.), *Bringing Problem-Based Learning to Higher Education: Theory and Practice*. San Francisco: Jossey-Bass, 1996.

Endemol. (Producer). *Extreme Makeover: Home Edition*. New York: ABC, 2003. Television series.

Fink, L. D. *Creating Significant Learning Experiences: An Integrated Approach to Designing College Courses*. San Francisco: Jossey-Bass, 2003.

JOAN M. NICOLL-SENFT *is an associate professor of special education at Central Connecticut State University. E-mail: nicoll-senftj@ccsu.edu.*

NEW DIRECTIONS FOR TEACHING AND LEARNING • DOI: 10.1002/tl

10

This chapter describes an engineering curriculum reform effort that threads a common four-year design theme across multiple courses within the curriculum.

Sooner City: Reflections on a Curriculum Reform Project

Randall L. Kolar, David A. Sabatini, K. K. Muraleetharan

In 1998, the School of Civil Engineering and Environmental science at the University of Oklahoma began implementing a curriculum reform project entitled "Sooner City—Design Across the Curriculum":

> For the project, incoming freshman are given a plat of land that is turned into a blueprint for critical infrastructure segments of the city. Design tasks include all facets of the traditional civil engineering program, ranging from sewer and water infrastructure to steel buildings. The project is unique in that it threads a common, four-year design theme throughout the curriculum. It also unifies the curriculum and allows material learned in early courses to carry forward. A primary goal is to produce graduates who consistently think at a higher level, and who are thus capable of handling open-ended design projects that require creativity, self-analysis, and awareness of economic, social, and political issues [Kolar, Muraleetharan, Mooney, and Vieux, 2000, p. 79].

Part of the motivation for the project was to transform the educational environment from passive to active learning and produce more broadly educated engineers capable of critical thinking. It is no coincidence that the project we undertook espoused many of the same goals presented in Dee Fink's book, *Creating Significant Learning Experiences* (2003); Dee had been a co-investigator on the Sooner City project, which was funded by the National Science Foundation, and helped formulate many of the learning objectives and the evaluation plan. But rather than focus on a specific

course, we applied Fink's concepts to the entire curriculum. In this chapter, we discuss the motivation for the project, the learning experiences realized by the project, and observations on the impact of the curriculum reform.

Background and Motivation for the Project

The Sooner City concept began several years before 1998 when we (along with other faculty in the department) began experimenting with alternative teaching techniques in individual courses. As a group, we were dissatisfied with the traditional way of doing business in the classroom. Engineering programs across the country, including ours, were stuck in a rut by following the same standard format: passive lectures on technical concepts followed by little or no classroom discussion, with individual homework on simplified problems, and problem-solving exams. Real-world design problems, if used at all, were introduced only in upper-level capstone courses.

Having been ourselves taught in this manner, and not having any formal instruction in alternative teaching techniques, we simply followed the same pattern when we became faculty members. Furthermore, the system did seem to produce competent civil engineering graduates. And so it was perpetuated, until a change agent, Dee Fink, shook up these established teaching traditions by challenging us to question everything we did in the classroom.

A critical analysis of our teaching techniques showed that we were not, in Fink's words, creating significant learning experiences through our traditional passive lectures. Moreover, a thorough examination of our curriculum showed that by artificially segregating the curriculum into independent units (courses) with little integration, we were inadvertently teaching our students that engineering topics are not interrelated. Thus, the traditional formula that had produced generations of competent design engineers was ill suited for producing graduates who can contribute in a dynamic, team-oriented environment and see the integrated nature of the civil engineering discipline.

Of equal concern was that the traditional system discouraged many talented students from pursuing engineering education; the attrition rate exceeds 40 percent at a number of leading institutions. Common reasons students leaving engineering cite include failing to see relevance in introductory classes and a lack of nurturing during the first two years of the curriculum.

External factors also drove the reexamination of our engineering curriculum, including a change in ABET accreditation criteria from counting credits in certain courses to an outcomes-based assessment; alumni and employers who were disappointed with the limited design skills of our graduates; and a push by our professional society, the American Society of Civil Engineers (2007), which outlines the body of knowledge that graduates should possess in order to enter the practice of civil engineering.

Thus, Sooner City was and remains our response to the need for classroom and curriculum reform. From a curriculum point of view, we believe that the best way to generate excitement and improve retention in engineer-

New Directions for Teaching and Learning • DOI: 10.1002/tl

ing is to introduce real-world design problems, with their concomitant political, economic, and environmental concerns, throughout the curriculum so that students can see the relevant application of theory. And from a classroom learning point of view, Sooner City provides a natural venue for alternative educational techniques, such as just-in-time learning (material is presented as needed in order to complete the particular design problem), collaborative learning (students work in teams on well-conceived design problems), and assessment through the use of learning portfolios (Kolar and Sabatini, 2004).

Transformational Educational Activities

We break down Sooner City activities into the six kinds of significant learning experiences that Fink identifies in his taxonomy of significant learning.

Foundational Knowledge

In the traditional curriculum, the majority of classroom time was spent providing foundational knowledge through passive lectures. As the name *foundational* implies, students must have this knowledge in order to advance in the discipline, but it should not be the definitive learning experience in the classroom. Rather, it should serve as the basis for stepping up to higher-level learning discussed under other components in the taxonomy. To provide time for these other kinds of learning, we embraced the readiness assurance process advocated by Michaelsen, Knight, and Fink (2004).

The basic philosophy behind team-based learning is to move much of the acquisition of foundational knowledge to out-of-classroom reading and self-study so that classroom activities can be reserved for higher-level learning. Student preparation is judged through the use of readiness assessment tests, affectionately known as RATs, which are short multiple-choice and true-false quizzes on the background reading materials. RATs are taken first individually and then in groups, helping to promote teamwork skills. By grading RATs in class or getting student feedback on responses, the instructor can determine which concepts the students understand well and which they are struggling with, thereby allowing the professor to focus precious class time on concepts the students struggle with, while offloading the acquisition of simpler concepts to the student on their own time. Having wrestled with the RAT answers individually and in their groups, students are especially alert to understanding the concepts discussed by the professor.

Learning How to Learn

The RATs are an important tool in teaching students how to learn on their own in that they are given to the students before any class discussion is devoted to the topic. Because a nontrivial portion of their grade is determined by RAT scores, the students must learn to learn on their own. We explain to the students that this mimics the workplace environment, where the employer

NEW DIRECTIONS FOR TEACHING AND LEARNING • DOI: 10.1002/tl

will expect junior engineers to learn simpler concepts on their own and approach their mentors only for explanations of more challenging concepts.

A second method that addresses this learning objective is the use of complex design problems that far exceed the problems typically found at the end of a chapter in a textbook. Thus, the students must resort to other sources of information (for example, the Web, other texts, engineering handbooks, and manufacturers' catalogues) to gather data and learn solution procedures. In addition, the students learn to sort through data and information given to them on these complex design projects and decide for themselves which ones are critical and which are trivial or redundant.

Application

A centerpiece of the Sooner City paradigm is that the design problems are drawn from complex, real-world examples, albeit centered around a virtual city instead of a real one. And design problems in engineering, by their very nature, force students to develop higher-level thinking skills. Design is an open-ended optimization problem in which students attempt to find the best solution subject to constraints we call design criteria. In theory, a given design problem has an infinite number of solutions, but the criteria constrain those to a more manageable number. Still, students must self-assess multiple alternatives, which forces them to develop this critical analysis skill. Yet at the same time, the open-endedness of the design problem allows students to be creative in proposing a solution. A common mantra in our design courses is that "there is no best solution." Nonetheless, some solutions are certainly better than others, so the students must learn to discern one from another. Many students find this lack of certainty unsettling, but it is precisely such an experience that advances their analysis skills. Finally, the use of real data promotes critical thinking because not all data are of the same quality and many times an engineer is confronted with the issue of having too many or too few data, so the students must learn to critically analyze the information they have.

Integration

Civil design projects are often constrained by many competing nontechnical challenges, such as environmental impacts, societal acceptance, economics, and political realities. A complete solution must effectively consider each and integrate those concerns into a final solution. Students work on components of the Sooner City project in multiple courses within a given semester and across all four years of their curriculum. Information is transferred between classes in the same semester and between semesters to help the students learn how all courses in the curriculum must be integrated to develop engineering solutions in complex systems.

Human Dimension

Our professional society advertises that civil engineering is a "people-serving profession," and indeed it is. Projects that students work on have an impact on every infrastructure aspect of civilization. Thus, by tying the product of the design work to society, students must tackle the human dimension of their work. In other words, how will the project affect the everyday lives of people? Another way that the curriculum promotes the human dimension of learning is through the liberal use of collaborative learning: students must develop people skills and learn to value the capabilities of their peers, as well as deal with their shortcomings.

In addition, the team building that occurs through the RAT and design process helps students learn about human dynamics. Students learn that a team that builds on and integrates the skills of the team members produces a product far superior to that which can be realized by the sum of the individual efforts. One example of such a lesson is the group RATs. Inevitably, at the beginning of the semester, some group RAT scores will be lower than the highest individual RAT score by a group member; that is, a group member was talked out of the right answer. Learning to prevent a dominant personality from stifling the creativity within a group is an important lesson in the human dimension and effective teamwork.

Caring

Our experience with the Sooner City paradigm is that students emerge from the program more connected to their profession than non–Sooner City students because they have a better appreciation of the importance of their discipline. When they realize the important contributions that they can make to society, their excitement and feeling of self-worth increase.

Impact on Student Learning

The evaluation plan for the project includes well-established techniques, such as formative and summative evaluations, and project-specific diagnostic tools. The evaluation activities are designed to collect information that provides data-based, criterion-referenced answers to the following questions:

Formative
- Is this project working as anticipated?
- Are any significant changes needed?

Summative
- Will the retention rate of Sooner City students be improved?
- Can the Sooner City students retain concepts and knowledge from previous courses?
- Can the Sooner City students apply these concepts to solve comprehensive design problems?

The primary mechanism to collect data is student and faculty interviews, but this is supplemented with performance on standardized tests and performance in the senior capstone design class (as compared to non–Sooner City students who enrolled in the curriculum before the project was implemented).

Following are eight highlights from the evaluation results set out in our final report to the National Science Foundation (Kolar, 2003):

1. Students had a better understanding of the design process.
2. Students experienced the interconnectedness and complexity of real-world design projects.
3. Students were better able to handle ambiguity and assess multiple alternatives.
4. There was a positive correlation between retention and the number of Sooner City credits taken.
5. Sooner City students showed, on average, a 6 percent higher year-to-year retention rate than other students in the College of Engineering.
6. Internship students (students who earn credit for working at local engineering firms) reported that the Sooner City curriculum was excellent preparation for actual design work and gave them the confidence to tackle complex designs that had many competing social, economic, and technical factors.
7. Faculty noted increased design capabilities among Sooner City students.
8. Faculty felt strongly that the project promoted design and cross-course integration in a flexible manner with minimal disruption to the curriculum.

Conclusion

The innovations inspired by our collaboration with Dee Fink have transformed the educational experience of our students from a passive, dull learning environment that actually turns many students off to engineering to an active, dynamic learning environment that inspires students and helps retain bright, creative students in the curriculum. As a result, today's graduates are much more prepared to assume leadership roles in engineering practice. While faculty effort is required to make this transition, this is offset by improved student learning and enthusiasm and the fact that teaching is much more fun.

We believe that the Sooner City project and Fink's ideas created an environment of educational excellence and innovations in integration of research and education within our whole department. The evidence for this excellence and innovation is five more National Science Foundation CAREER awards and two National Science Foundation GK–12 (Graduate Teaching Fellows in K–12 Education) awards for our faculty. This number of awards for a single department is one of the highest per capita rates in the whole country.

Receiving awards for our endeavors is of course deeply satisfying, but our greatest sense of accomplishment comes from the quality and competence we see in our students when they graduate as civil engineers.

References

American Society of Civil Engineers. "Academic Prerequisites for Licensure and Professional Practice." ASCE Policy Statement 465. 2007. Retrieved Oct. 18, 2008, from http://www.asce.org/pressroom/news/policy_details.cfm?hdlid=15.

Fink, L. D. *Creating Significant Learning Experiences: An Integrated Approach to Designing College Courses.* San Francisco: Jossey-Bass, 2003.

Kolar, R. L. "Sooner City—Design Across the Curriculum: Final Project Report." National Science Foundation, Award 9872505, Dec. 2003.

Kolar, R. L., Muraleetharan, K. K., Mooney, M. A., and Vieux, B. E. "Sooner City—Design Across the Curriculum." *Journal of Engineering Education,* 2000, 89(1), 79–87.

Kolar, R. L., and Sabatini, D. A. "Use of Reflective Writing/Learning Portfolios in a Junior-Level Water Resources Engineering Class." In J. Zubizarreta (ed.), *The Learning Portfolio: Reflective Practice for Improving Student Learning.* San Francisco: Anker/Jossey-Bass, 2004.

Michaelsen, L. K., Knight, A. B., and Fink, L. D. *Team-Based Learning: A Transformative Use of Small Groups.* Sterling, Va.: Stylus, 2004.

RANDALL L. KOLAR is the Austin Presidential Professor in the School of Civil Engineering and Environmental Science (CEES) at the University of Oklahoma and serves as the associate director of the OU WaTER Center and the Center for Natural Disasters and Hazard Research, which is affiliated with the National Weather Center. E-mail: kolar@ou.edu.

DAVID A. SABATINI is a David Ross Boyd Professor at the University of Oklahoma and holds the Sun Oil Company Endowed Chair in CEES and is the director of the OU WaTER Center. E-mail: sabatini@ou.edu.

K. K. MURALEETHARAN is a President's Associates Presidential Professor in CEES at the University of Oklahoma and a Fellow of the American Society of Civil Engineers. E-mail: muralee@ou.edu.

11

In 2007, Fink taught a graduate-level course, Preparing for College-Level Teaching, at the University of Oklahoma. This experience generated three specific lessons worth sharing.

Still Learning

L. Dee Fink

My book on integrated course design was published in 2003, and two years later I retired from the University of Oklahoma, in part to free myself up to respond to the requests that started coming from other campuses to do faculty workshops on this topic. However, one of the carry-over commitments at Oklahoma was to teach a graduate course on college teaching in the College of Engineering as part of a grant that had been received just before I retired. This chapter shares some lessons that I learned from the last time I taught that course in 2007.

Background Information

As ironic as it may seem, teaching this course was a daunting experience, not because of the subject or the students but because of the larger context. If you have published a nationally visible book on college teaching and you are going around the country running workshops on how to teach, and then you actually teach, it had better be good, and it had better look and feel different from most other courses.

My awareness of this situation led me to do two things. First, I quite consciously tried to follow my own advice. In planning the course, I tried to carefully and systematically follow my own recommendations. Second, I also tried to push the envelope a bit. Were there ideas I had learned from my workshop interactions with faculty after the publication of the book? Were there new and creative ways of applying the general principles laid out in the book?

NEW DIRECTIONS FOR TEACHING AND LEARNING, no. 119, Fall 2009 © Wiley Periodicals, Inc.
Published online in Wiley InterScience (www.interscience.wiley.com) • DOI: 10.1002/tl.369

Three New Ideas

In retrospect, three new ideas emerged on designing college courses that seem worth sharing with others.

Identify the Big Purpose of the Course

In my book, I recommended starting the design process by gathering information about situational factors and then developing a set of specific, significant learning goals. This is still good advice. But when I had worked with individual faculty members who had attended my workshop, we often spent time developing a new, more ambitious vision of what I have subsequently come to call the big purpose of the course. This involves standing back from the course and looking at where the students are coming from and how they might use the ideas from the course in their personal, professional, social, and civic lives after graduation. Once the teacher has a clearer, richer sense of the big purpose of the course, then she or he can go on to develop specific learning goals.

Three brief examples may give some concrete meaning to the concept of the big purpose of a course. One teacher I worked with was teaching a course about prisons in a criminal justice program. Before our discussion, the course primarily provided information about how prisons are managed for students who wanted to get jobs working in a prison. After our discussion, he developed the idea of having the course examine prison operations from three macroperspectives: those working in prisons, the people being handled by prisons (that is, the inmates), and citizens who needed a way for society to handle antisocial behavior in a way that was both cost-effective and just. The course could then prompt students to ask: "How should a prison system work if you examine it separately from each of these three perspectives?"

In a second example, a teacher had a course about mass media. Before our discussion, she primarily focused on providing information about how each of the major media (radio, TV, journals, and newspapers) worked. After our discussion, she decided a bigger purpose would be to have students work toward conducting a comparative analysis of how major news events are handled by each of the major media. What aspects of news did they handle well or not so well, given the processes by which they generated news stories?

A third professor taught a course on consumer finance. After our discussion, he decided to focus on helping students not only acquire knowledge about financial issues but also to develop confidence in their ability to handle any future financial decision—for example, taking a loan to buy a house, choosing among various retirement options, setting up savings and investment plans, or financing college for their children.

When I came back to my course at Oklahoma, my view of the situational factors was as follows. This course would be the only formal preparation these students would get for their roles as teaching professors in higher education. Therefore, I wanted it to prepare them widely for this role. In addition to learning how to teach their own courses, I wanted to prepare them to participate in the larger organizational contexts in which they would be working and to contribute positively to improving those various organizational contexts.

Given this view of the link between this course and their future lives as teaching academics, I created the statement in Exhibit 11.1 about the big purpose of this course that I put in the course syllabus. Then, based on this view of the big purpose of the course, I generated the major learning goals as shown in Exhibit 11.2. These goals are obviously built around my taxonomy of significant learning. But they also can be seen as spelling out the learning implications of the big purpose that I had chosen for this course.

Have Students Build the Evaluation Rubric for Major Projects

This course had a number of major projects, some of which were done individually and others by groups. One of the group projects was to design a course. Since these students were nearly all in engineering, we identified a common course in engineering that they had taken and might likely teach in the future.

Again trying to follow my own advice about feedback and assessment, I wanted to set up the project so students could engage in self-assessment at the end of it. But to do this, they needed to know what constituted appropriate criteria and standards: they needed an assessment rubric.

When it came time for them to start working on this project, it occurred to me to have the students develop the assessment rubric themselves rather than for me to give it to them. So I went to the whiteboard and

Exhibit 11.1 The Big Purpose of This Course

General Purpose and Course Goals

The general purpose of this course is to provide graduate students with a strong preparation for their future role as professional educators at the college and university level.

In my view, a person is well prepared to be a college teacher if they can DO the following:

1. Build a sophisticated philosophy of teaching.
2. Develop some basic skills and capabilities, for example, an ability to:
    a. Design powerful learning experiences.
    b. Assess different kinds of student learning.
    c. Create good assignments for learning groups.
    d. Lead classroom activities effectively.
    e. Evaluate your own teaching.
3. Create a professional development plan.
4. Know how to operate in and be an advocate for change (as appropriate) in multiple organizational contexts: departments, institutions, and disciplinary associations.
5. Identify changes occurring in the nature of the professoriate in higher education (and their implications for pedagogy, the professoriate, and so forth).

NEW DIRECTIONS FOR TEACHING AND LEARNING • DOI: 10.1002/tl

Exhibit 11. 2 The Specific Learning Goals for This Course

My hope as a teacher of this course is that, by the end of the course, everyone will . . .

1. Have a good knowledge of:
   a. Several major ideas in the literature on college teaching
   b. Multiple resources for learning about teaching
2. Know how to perform several key tasks in teaching:
   c. Develop a sophisticated philosophy of teaching and learning
   d. Design courses
   e. Create effective assignments for learning groups
   f. Evaluate student learning
   g. Exercise leadership in the classroom
   h. Evaluate your own teaching
3. Identify the interactions between:
   i. Oneself, the subject, students, and life
   j. Oneself as a teacher, the institution in which one teaches, the discipline in which you work
4. Develop one's human capabilities:
   k. Confidence in your ability to teach well
   l. Ability to interact with others (students, colleagues, administrators)
5. Value:
   m. High-quality teaching and learning
   n. Continuous growth as a professional educator
6. Monitor and direct your own professional development:
   o. Create a learning portfolio
   p. Create a teaching portfolio
   q. Create a plan for your own professional development as a teacher

asked, "Based on what you have learned thus far about designing courses, what should be the criteria for a good course design?" After they had identified the main criteria, I asked them to identify standards of high-quality work for each criterion.

In this process, I essentially led the discussion: writing their answers on the whiteboard and helping organize and clarify their answers. I was prepared to add any criteria and standards that they did not generate. But as it turned out, they identified all the major criteria and formulated good standards for each one.

So in my mind, we had prepared them to do the self-assessment activity at the end of the project. What I was not prepared for was the extraordinarily high quality of work that the groups presented at the end of the project. All three groups did exceptionally good work. To be sure, they were in general good students. I had had good students before, but the work in previous classes was not so uniformly good across all groups.

I concluded that what accounted for this high level of performance was having the students build the assessment rubric before they did the project. In the process of developing the rubric, they also developed their own expectations of what they needed to do during the project. They were self-assessing all the way through the project, not just at the end.

The major lesson from this experience was this. After you have completed a major unit of study but before students start a culminating project, have them use what they have learned to develop the assessment rubric for the project. This activity will prepare them to engage in self-assessment at the end of the project and will also raise the quality of their work during the doing of the project.

Create a String of Activities

In my book, I discussed the importance of making sure the course design is integrated and mentioned two ways of doing this: using the three-column table and choosing a powerful teaching strategy. During this course, I discovered another integration procedure that I called a string of activities.

One of my major goals for this course was to prepare students for continuing to learn about college teaching throughout their academic career. There are numerous ideas in the literature on college teaching—many more than we had time to study in this course. One of my major goals was for students to learn how to put themselves on a growth curve in terms of learning about teaching. Therefore, one of the major projects near the end of the course was for them to develop a plan for their own future learning about teaching and to put this plan into both a teaching and a learning portfolio.

Although I had included this assignment in previous versions of this course, I had not created a sequence, or string of activities, that built up to the task of creating such a plan, step by step. Here is the string of activities that I created for this course.

- Week 3: "Look for and bring to class a list of resources for identifying topics about college teaching." This might be, for example, Web sites, bibliographies, or the reference sections from books on teaching. After students turned these in, we noted how varied and different each list was. Then we compiled and distributed a master list of all the resources.
- Week 5: "Using the master list of resources, identify ten to fifteen topics about college teaching beyond the ones we will study in this course." I wanted the students to realize that the literature on college teaching has many powerful ideas and that we are studying only a select few of these. Again, they came back with lists of different topics, so we compiled and distributed a master list of those topics.
- Week 7: "Review the master list of topics, and identify four topics that you consider most urgent for you to learn about in the next one to three years." They were to write a short statement about why they considered these four topics to be particularly important for them to learn about.
- Week 9: "Select one of these four topics and learn about it right now—on your own, outside of class." This might be done by reading a book about

the topic, watching someone do something, interviewing a professor about what he or she was doing, or trying something themselves if they were teaching. This was essentially an independent learning project.

- Week 11: "Turn in your report about your independent learning project." In this report, they summarized why they had chosen that topic, described what they did to learn about it, and summarized what they had learned about it. After they had turned their reports in, I commented to them: "Notice what you have just done. You have proved to yourself that you are capable of learning about college-level teaching, on your own, without me, without a course. You are capable of being independent, self-directed learners." For many, this was a major realization.

- Week 13: "For each of the other three topics on your short list, identify an appropriate learning strategy." Once they had finished this, they had the major elements of a plan for future learning. They had identified what they wanted or needed to learn (a learning agenda) and appropriate ways of learning about each topic (learning strategies).

- Week 15 (the final week of the course): "Now, take your plan for future learning, and put it in as the final section of both your end-of-course projects: your teaching portfolio and your learning portfolio."

As a result of having this string of activities in the course, all students developed a plan in which they had learned how to find resources, developed a long list of possible topics on teaching, formulated a short list of urgent topics for reasons distinctive to themselves, had proven to themselves that they were capable of independent learning, and had identified learning strategies for the three remaining topics. My expectation is that the likelihood they will act on their plans is quite high because each was self-generated and they now had confidence that they could learn on their own.

What I Learned

I learned three major lessons from this teaching experience.

The first is that the framework for designing significant learning experiences presented in my book still seems valid, although I would now note the value of identifying the big purpose of a course near the front of the design process.

Second, I discovered some additional procedures for applying the general principles that made the design process even stronger. In this case, those procedures involved having students build the evaluation rubric for assessing their own work before doing a culminating project for a unit within the course and creating a string of activities that build up to major culminating projects for the course.

Third, and perhaps most important, no matter how much one might know about teaching or even about a specific aspect of teaching such as

designing courses, it is always possible to learn even more and get even better. This means that for all of us, learning how to be a better teacher is a
process that will never end. Learning how to teach well will be a continuous, career-long learning challenge.

L. DEE FINK *founded and directed the Instructional Development Program at the
University of Oklahoma from 1979 until 2005. He currently works as a national
and international consultant on instruction in higher education.*

NEW DIRECTIONS FOR TEACHING AND LEARNING • DOI: 10.1002/tl

This chapter reviews the preceding chapters and distills from that collection answers to three questions that all good teachers need to ask and answer.

Lessons We Can Learn from the Voices of Experience

Arletta Knight Fink, L. Dee Fink

The preceding chapters in this volume have been written by teachers who have used the ideas of integrated course design (ICD) in an effort to improve their teaching and their students' learning. They represent a variety of disciplines and different levels of teaching experience. Their disciplines come from the full spectrum of university departments: music, accounting, virology, philosophy, art history, Spanish, economics, civil engineering, psychology, biology, special education, and biomolecular sciences. Some of these teachers are in the early years of their careers as college teachers, and others are veterans.

The purpose of this chapter is to explore what we can all learn from their experiences. In pursuing this goal, we organize these lessons around three questions that everyone who teaches are likely to be curious about:

1. *Can it be done?* That is, is it possible to change one's teaching in a way that makes a discernible and substantial difference in what and how students learn?
2. *What does it take to make that happen?* What did these teachers have to do to make such a difference happen?
3. *Will it benefit us, the teachers, as well as our students?* If we make the effort to change the way we teach, will it have any benefit for us as well?

Let's see what their experiences tell us.

NEW DIRECTIONS FOR TEACHING AND LEARNING, no. 119, Fall 2009 © Wiley Periodicals, Inc.
Published online in Wiley InterScience (www.interscience.wiley.com) • DOI: 10.1002/tl.370

Can It Be Done?

The "it" in this question refers to teachers' changing the design of their courses in a way that leads to a major, discernible difference in the learning of their students. And the answer to this question is a resounding, "Yes, it can be done." All of these teachers report that this new way of designing their courses did result in major, discernible differences in the way their students responded.

Given the widespread skepticism throughout the professoriate about the possibility of any genuine, substantive improvement in the results of our teaching, this is no small finding. Professors everywhere bemoan the seemingly inevitable results of "no significant difference" found at the end of so many educational studies.

In contrast, the authors in this volume came to a very different conclusion. Their efforts to change both their own teaching and their students' learning made a significant difference in two important ways: greater student engagement and more significant kinds of learning.

Greater Student Engagement

The first thing that has to happen in any instructional situation is the students have to be motivated to spend the energy necessary to do the work of learning. Sometimes they come at least partially motivated; more often, the teacher has to help them find that motivation.

Essentially all the teachers who redesigned their courses reported greater student excitement and motivation. Rose and Torosyan echoed what many other professors in this volume said about greater student involvement: "Energy in the classroom increased significantly when there was less lecturing and increased group work and discussion. . . . [In fact] the new energy was palpable."

It is also exciting when the students themselves are aware of and share their thoughts on how the course has affected their motivation. Students in Huber's courses reflect the feelings and thoughts of many students when they commented: "This is one of the best classes I have ever taken; I will be able to use the knowledge in the future; I learned to do somebody's taxes without my professor's help!" and "The projects you assigned helped me learn the material way better than any lecture could ever do."

More Significant Student Learning

As important as student motivation and engagement are, we also want that energy to result in a kind of learning that we, the students, and others can look at and say, "Yes, that is significant!" Fink's taxonomy offers a conceptual framework for identifying significant kinds of learning. To what degree did significant learning occur in these redesigned courses and curricula? The chapters included both quantitative and qualitative data on this question.

Quantitative Data. Fallahi and her colleagues offer some of the best quantitative data available so far on this question. This group conducted a meta-analysis of their individual assessments. Data reveal significant improvement in student learning and abilities across their various disciplines. They found improvement that was statistically significant (at the .05 level of significance) in foundation knowledge, application, the human dimension, and learning how to learn. Although the data were positive but not statistically significant across all six courses for the other two kinds of significant learning (integration and caring), data from three of their courses showed a significant improvement in integration, and one course showed a significant improvement in caring. The most vital piece of information from this meta-analysis was that redesigning courses using ICD made a measurable improvement in all six categories of Fink's taxonomy.

Fayne also had quantitative data to report. Recently her courses had received mediocre ratings on student engagement and student learning. After redesigning her class using ICD, her data revealed that 96 percent of the students believed that the course was challenging, 83 percent believed that they had been required to think independently and creatively, and 87 percent believed they had learned a great deal. There had also been a major shift in attitudes toward the course between the start and end of the course. The precourse survey revealed that 74 percent of students started with a neutral or negative attitude toward the course. At its conclusion, 83 percent of the students had a "very positive" or positive attitude, and only 2 percent indicated a neutral attitude. No student indicated having a negative attitude.

Qualitative Data. Mester used a table to describe, for each of the six components of Fink's taxonomy, the impact of specific changes on student learning. For example, by giving students more open-ended kinds of problems and challenging them to find creative solutions, student performance on problem-solving assessment activities became much more creative.

In general, the contributing professors found that what students learn in the classroom is most effective when it relates to the students in a personal way and when the students can relate their learning to the world outside the classroom. Essentially all the chapter authors reported success in this regard; we have included some of the results they reported in the statements below:

- Davis: Students learned Spanish well enough to converse with native speakers for an entire evening at a Mexican restaurant.
- Kolar, Sabatini, and Muraleetharan: Students developed higher-level thinking skills as a result of solving authentic, not fabricated, design problems taken from real situations.
- Kelley: The redesign of his class gave students the chance to think more deeply about, and be creative with, the special relationship of music, text, and performance.

- Rose and Torosyan: Students made the big questions meaningful and applied course content to real-world observations.
- Faynes: Students not only acquired knowledge but were motivated to use it.

The answer to our question "Can it be done?" is clearly a resounding "yes." These authors were very successful in finding ways to redesign their courses and curricula that generated greater student engagement and more significant student learning.

What Does It Take to Make That Happen?

The second question we posed is: What did these professors have to do to achieve the kinds of results they did? The answer should facilitate the efforts the rest of us might want to make to achieve similar results.

It turns out there were several things they did, and all seem to be important to their ability to achieve positive results. We describe five factors that were important to their success and we present them in the order in which they need to happen.

Willingness to Look Critically at What They (and Their Colleagues) Were Currently Doing

The vast majority of college teachers have had no formal preparation for their roles and responsibilities as professional educators. As a result, what they do in most cases is teach the way they were taught: they continue the traditional ways of teaching in their respective disciplines.

However, the chapter authors in this volume had something in them that made them dissatisfied with what they saw happening when they followed their traditional models. Although their teaching may have been judged satisfactory by status quo criteria, they felt unsatisfied with the levels of student engagement and the quality of student learning they saw. Rose and Torosyan, for example, commented, "We had both been dissatisfied with our students' learning outcomes and our own tired patterns of teaching." Fayne was disheartened by the increase in "lukewarm" ratings regarding students' perceptions of their own learning and engagement. And Mester believed there was "room for improvement" in regard to student learning. He was especially concerned about students' long-term knowledge retention.

Davis was well aware that her students' failure to succeed was blatantly obvious: "Despite the time spent in class, they had little to show for their effort and were unable to speak the language." Miners and Nantz had been unable to engage their students in the course material even though they had been working for several years to revitalize their classes. Their conclusion was that if they wanted quality student learning, they were going to have to make a different kind of change in order to transform their teaching.

New Directions for Teaching and Learning • DOI: 10.1002/tl

Willingness to Search Widely for New and Better Ideas on Teaching and Learning

Most professors, if they are honest about it, will not say they are deeply satisfied with the current quality of student learning. However, the difference between most professors and the chapter authors is that the latter were not willing to simply blame the students. Nor did they throw up their hands in frustration and resign themselves to the view that it is not possible to do any better. They had a deep commitment to finding a better way to teach. They took the view articulated so nicely by Miners and Nantz: if we want our students to change, we have to be ready to change.

To accomplish this, they did the fairly obvious things. They spent time attending workshops, reading books, and talking to colleagues who had learned about and tried new ideas. This is the kind of professional development that occurs routinely in law, medicine, commercial aviation, and other professions. Unfortunately this has not yet become a routine activity in college teaching, but it needs to be, as the experiences of these professors attest.

Using the New Ideas They Found, Faithfully and Responsibly

Whenever practicing professionals encounter a good new idea, they have to learn how to implement that idea faithfully and responsibly. That is, they cannot just learn about it and then do something somewhat like it but ignore the essential principles of that idea.

In this case, there were two new ideas: significant learning (the goal) and integrated course design (the method of achieving the goal). These authors did an excellent job of following the basic procedures of redesigning their courses for more significant learning: they analyzed the situational factors, formulated significant learning goals, used the principles of active learning and educative assessment in generating appropriate learning activities and assessment activities, borrowed or created a powerful teaching strategy. As they did this, there were two general lessons that have wide applicability.

The Value of ICD for Achieving Significant Learning.   The authors often reported that the process of creating new learning goals using Fink's taxonomy allowed them to dream more widely and gave them a language to make explicit what they yearned for implicitly. While traditional ways of teaching have tended to center on two learning goals, foundational knowledge and basic application, Fink's taxonomy opens up a new world of learning goals by including integration, human dimension, caring, and learning how to learn. Several chapter authors commented on the value of this enlarged scope of possible learning goals:

- Kolar, Sabatini, and Muraleetharan in civil engineering experienced success in a discipline not typically associated with caring and the human dimension. They observed that students' feelings of self-worth and excitement with their chosen profession were heightened when they realized the valuable contributions they could make to society. The students emerged from their program feeling a genuine connection to their profession.

- Mester commented that although the human dimension and caring are "often overlooked in the scientific curriculum, [they] were powerful motivators and integrators."
- Huber was especially intrigued about caring because this dimension is not ordinarily associated with accounting. She was delighted to discover that students were not only learning the course material, but were also showing evidence of caring about their chosen professions by developing professional mind-sets.

These authors said that the ideas of ICD gave them the tools they needed to work with a new level of intentionality and achieve this valued kind of learning. Kelley wrote: "I have always intuitively wanted my students to experience the types of significant learning that Fink identified . . . but I lacked the design structure." Fallahi and her colleagues echoed the same sentiment: "All of us wanted to make changes to our courses but had never [before] had a structure to help us accomplish these goals."

Involving Students in Shaping the Course. Several professors noted the positive response of students when they made the students partners in the process of creating powerful learning experiences. This reflects the claim that Weimer (2002) made some years ago about the positive results of sharing our power as teachers with our students:

- Miners and Nantz asked their students to self-assess the progress of their own learning.
- Many authors reported asking students to reflect on their learning by writing about their individual learning experiences in papers, journal entries, or student learning portfolios. Thinking about one's own learning encourages students to accept ownership and move toward becoming a meta-learner.
- Mester went one step further when he involved his students in creating course objectives, exams, and assessment rubrics.
- Davis noted that her students had never before been asked to consider their own learning goals.
- Fink was impressed by the consistently high-quality work that resulted when he asked students to generate the assessment rubric for a major assignment rather than him just giving it to them.

Creatively Adapting New Ideas to Their Situation and Subject Matter

This may seem to be the opposite of the preceding lesson, but it is really a necessary complement. When implementing a new idea, teachers need to adhere to the essential principles of that idea. But any new idea also has to be adapted to the specific situation and subject matter, and this often calls for some creativity. There are numerous examples of creativity in these chapters—for example:

- Kelley created a new exercise, the Pretty Polly project, which challenged students to go beyond just understanding the compositional architecture of songs to changing that architecture to reflect a more direct relationship to the lyrics.
- Huber, in her shoebox exercise, reported the flash of insight when she asked herself: "Why don't I have the students create the tax cases rather than me creating them?"
- Fink came up with the novel idea of creating a string of activities throughout the semester that would prepare students for a major culminating project: creating a learning plan for their own near-future professional development.

Persistence

There are numerous examples of these professors doing what all innovators must do: persist past initial problems to see the idea through. Rose and Torosyan, for example, refer to "bumps and dead-ends" along the way. With major innovations, there are usually multiple subtasks that must be learned and be done properly if the innovation is to work. That is true with integrated course design as well.

All of our contributing professors had to learn how to write good learning goals using the taxonomy, create appropriate learning activities and assessment activities using the three-column table, create or borrow a powerful teaching strategy, and so forth. But they worked at these tasks and eventually made the ideas work—with extraordinary benefits for their students.

To review our answer to this second question, to achieve major improvements in teaching and learning, we must have (or develop) an attitude that prompts us to look critically at the results of our current teaching, be ready to spend the time and effort to learn new ideas, implement the new ideas faithfully while adapting them to the particular teaching situation, and be persistent in finding what it takes to make the new ideas work effectively.

Will It Benefit Us, the Teachers, as Well as Our Students?

It is all well and good to do something that benefits our students. But unless we, too, can realize some benefit, the time and energy costs may be greater than we are willing or able to pay.

As we first read these chapters, we heard two recurring themes from the authors about the benefits of this way of teaching for them.

A Renewed Joy in Teaching. Remarks such as "transformed my career" and "changed my life" reaffirmed our belief that there are many fringe benefits attached to the use of ICD. One of the most rewarding of those is the new joy in teaching that these professors are experiencing. Huber states that she "found a joy in teaching" that is not dependent on accolades from others. It is instead a joy that comes from the changes within herself and her courses. She writes that her "passion for teaching has been invigorated as she [continues to] hone her craft."

Kolar, Sabatini, and Muraleetharan write that ICD has transformed the entire educational experience for students as well as themselves. The students' learning experience has moved from a passive and dull environment to one that is "active and dynamic." As a result, "teaching is much more fun."

When thinking about the impact that ICD had on his class, Kelley reports that "it is in many ways the most rewarding course I have taught." Rose and Torosyan remark that they "experienced a sense of continuing renewal in our teaching energies."

Scholarship of Teaching and Learning. In addition to finding a new joy in teaching, several of the contributing professors also discovered an expansion of their professional careers in the form of contributing to the scholarship of teaching and learning. Because ICD had such a profound impact on each of their classes, many of them began to share their enthusiasm with their colleagues. Huber, for instance, writes that she could "hardly contain her excitement" as she told her colleagues about her first crack at creating a new course design.

The enthusiasm of our contributing authors, coupled with sharing their successes with their colleagues, led to more widespread and structured presentations on home campuses. The ever widening circle of workshops and presentations on ICD soon spread outside individual campuses, and new careers blossomed in the scholarship of teaching and learning. These new careers led to teaching seminars on course design, presenting at national conventions, and publishing papers and articles.

Along with workshops and presentations, Fallahi and her five colleagues were the inspiration for the development of a colloquium attended by fifty university faculty and administrators. Huber has been a featured speaker at numerous national events and has published extensively; Kolar, Sabatini, and Muraleetharan have several teaching and research awards. Clearly ICD generates excitement, enthusiasm, and an urge to share the word.

Conclusion

Coediting this volume of *New Directions for Teaching and Learning* has been one of the most delightful, as well as one of the most arduous, tasks, we have ever undertaken. The delight came from reading the inspirational chapters written by the contributing professors. The ardor came from having to be selective with what we shared in this chapter. There were so many great examples and so many terrific quotations that it was agonizingly difficult to make final decisions.

These professors have done a fantastic job of sharing the transformation of their teaching. Their concern about and commitment to the quality of teaching and learning in their individual courses rings out loud and clear. It is obvious that they have truly invested themselves in the process. As a result, all of us who read this book are the beneficiaries of their investment.

While we can each enjoy the success and satisfaction of our individual achievements in the classroom, a recurring theme across these chapters is the need for collective dialogue and assistance. All of these authors are well aware of the help they received along the way as they sought to enhance the learning experiences of their students. Now they are sharing what they have learned with those who are ready to embark on a journey of continuous improvement.

As teachers, our efforts are analogous to the collaborative efforts of those who attempt to climb mountains. If promoting significant learning is our mountain, the assent is more likely to be successful if we all pull together to reach the summit.

Reference

Weimer, M. *Learner-Centered Teaching*. San Francisco: Jossey-Bass, 2002.

ARLETTA KNIGHT FINK *served as associate director of the Instructional Development Program at the University of Oklahoma from 1992 until 2002.*

L. DEE FINK *founded and directed the Instructional Development Program at the University of Oklahoma from 1979 until 2005. He currently works as a national and international consultant on instruction in higher education.*

INDEX

Page references followed by *t* indicate a table; followed by *fig* indicate an illustrated figure; followed by *e* indicate an exhibit.

Why Wait to Make Great Discoveries

When you can make them in an instant with Wiley InterScience® Pay-Per-View and ArticleSelect™

Now you can have instant, full-text access to an extensive collection of journal articles or book chapters available on Wiley InterScience. With Pay-Per-View and ArticleSelect™, there's no limit to what you can discover...

ArticleSelect™ is a token-based service, providing access to full-text content from non-subscribed journals to existing institutional customers (EAL and BAL)

Pay-per-view is available to any user, regardless of whether they hold a subscription with Wiley InterScience.

Benefits:

- Access online full-text content from journals and books that are outside your current library holdings
- Use it at home, on the road, from anywhere at any time
- Build an archive of articles and chapters targeted for your unique research needs
- Take advantage of our free profiled alerting service the perfect companion to help you find specific articles in your field as soon as they're published
- Get what you need instantly no waiting for document delivery
- Fast, easy, and secure online credit card processing for pay-per-view downloads
- Special, cost-savings for EAL customers: whenever a customer spends tokens on a title equaling 115% of its subscription price, the customer is auto-subscribed for the year
- Access is instant and available for 24 hours

WILEY InterScience®
DISCOVER SOMETHING GREAT

www.interscience.wiley.com

4760